SPEAKING A NEW CLASSICISM:

AMERICAN ARCHITECTURE NOW

Smith College Museum of Art,
Northampton, Massachusetts   April 30–July 12, 1981

Sterling and Francine Clark Art Institute,
Williamstown, Massachusetts   July 25–September 8, 1981

D1264955

1. Peterson and Littenberg, *Les Halles Quarter*, 1979, cat. 98.

SPEAKING A NEW CLASSICISM:

AMERICAN ARCHITECTURE NOW

With essays by
Guest Curator, Helen Searing and
Henry Hope Reed

SMITH COLLEGE MUSEUM OF ART, NORTHAMPTON, MASSACHUSETTS

Curator of the exhibition: Helen Searing
Exhibition officer: Charles Chetham
Exhibition coordinators: Martha Krom
                         Michael Goodison
Exhibition design: Charles Chetham
                   David Dempsey
Editorial: Patricia Anderson   Martha Krom
           Charles Chetham   Linda Muehlig
           Michael Goodison   Helen Searing
           Betsy B. Jones   Kathryn Woo
Catalogue design: Charles Chetham
                  Linda Muehlig
Design consultant: John Lancaster
Type: Garamond
Printed in the USA by The Pioneer Valley Printing Company,
Easthampton, Massachusetts

Published by the Smith College Museum of Art, Northampton, Mas-
sachusetts with the aid of funds provided by the National Endowment for
the Arts, Washington, D.C., a federal agency and from Mrs. William A.
Evans, Jr. (Charlotte Cushman '29), Philip Johnson, Mrs. James E.
Pollak (Mabel Brown '27), Mrs. T. V. Searing, Mr. and Mrs. Morton I.
Sosland (Estelle Glatt '46), Mrs. Alfred R. Stern (Joanne Melniker '44),
Enid Silver Winslow (Enid Silver '54) and Museum Members, Smith
College Museum of Art.

Distributed worldwide by The University of Chicago Press, Chicago, Illinois

Photographs illustrated in the catalogue have been provided by the architects. Photographers are cited as follows:

Tom Bernard, Philadelphia, figs. 42–44
Orlando R. Cabanban, Chicago, fig. 28
Tom Crane, Bryn Mawr, fig. 20
Courtesy, Forbes Library, Northampton, Massachusetts, fig. 23
Robert L. Harper, figs. 17, 46
Norman McGrath, New York, figs. 19, 48
Courtesy, The Mount Vernon Ladies' Association, fig. 22
Richard Oliver, fig. 37
Thomas Gordon Smith, fig. 29
Jack Ward, New York, fig. 38
Tom Yee, Courtesy, *House and Garden* © 1981 by the Condé Nast
Publications, Inc., fig. 18

Cover: Moore, *Sammis Hall,* 1980, cat. 78.
End Papers: Venturi, *Knoll International Ceiling,* 1979, cat. 137.

TABLE OF CONTENTS

ARCHITECTS

Thomas H. Beeby

John Blatteau

Peter L. Gluck

Michael Graves

Allan Greenberg

Robert Harper

Philip Johnson

Robert Michael Kliment & Frances Halsband

Edward Levin

Rodolfo Machado & Jorge Silvetti

Henry L. Meltzer

Charles W. Moore

Christopher Morris & Timothy Morris

Richard B. Oliver

Stephen K. Peterson & Barbara Littenberg

James Stewart Polshek

Thomas Gordon Smith

Robert A. M. Stern

Stanley Tigerman

Robert Venturi, John Rauch & Denise Scott Brown

LENDERS

In addition to the architects listed, Gillian and Neil Levine, Brookline, Massachusetts, the Max Protetch Gallery, New York City, and Nan Swid of the same city are lenders to this exhibition.

ACKNOWLEDGMENTS

In the early spring of 1980 Helen Searing, who teaches art and architecture from the eighteenth through the twentieth centuries in the Art Department at Smith, proposed that the Smith College Museum of Art hold an exhibition focused on the renewed interest by architects in classical forms. Following our regular practice, she who proposes, if also expert, becomes guest curator of the exhibition and then works in tandem with members of the Museum staff who share an interest in the project. Professor Searing is an acute observer of architecture in its earlier manifestations and in its contemporary developments. In this she follows in the footsteps of her illustrious predecessors at Smith, Henry-Russell Hitchcock and William L. MacDonald. Ms. Searing also organized and moderated a symposium held at Smith on Saturday, May 9, 1981 which included Michael Graves, Allan Greenberg, James Stewart Polshek and Robert A. M. Stern, architects whose works are shown in this exhibition.

The exhibition became a reality through the efforts of a large number of people. Every exhibition requires special skills and the Museum at Smith College is fortunate in having talented people on its staff to make the aspirations of a guest curator a reality. Two "staff" members had particular responsibility for this exhibition. Martha Krom bore the brunt of coordinating the numerous communications among curator, director and architects. Michael Goodison's organizational abilities were pressed into service for the catalogue and many other related activities. Both work here at the Museum as National Endowment for the Arts Interns. In a seamless garment of compliments we know not whether it is appropriate to thank them for being available for subvention by the National Endowment for the Arts or to thank the NEA for subventing them. Both messages, of course, are to the point. In translating the exhibition from thought to fact all members of the staff were, so to speak, part of the designing and construction crew. Patricia Anderson, David Dempsey, Betsy B. Jones and Linda Muehlig have been listed elsewhere in this publication. Behind the scenes we commend Kathryn Woo, Assistant for Administration for the Museum, who oversees our requests for aid to the National Endowment for the Arts and ever after keeps us on the financial straight and narrow; Constance Ellis who sees that the information about the exhibition is distributed and that our social obligations are met with good form; Drusilla Kuschka who types our unreadable manuscripts; William MacRae of Pioneer Valley Printing who gets a catalogue out splendidly no matter what the deadline.

In the course of every exhibition, the Museum is assisted by many people whose help whether large or small is crucial to the project. Henry Hope Reed, the distinguished critic of architecture and the defender of classicism throughout the hegemony of the International Style, was recommended to us by Robert A. M. Stern to write one of the catalogue essays. Mr. Stern also suggested architects for inclusion in the exhibition. These gentlemen together with the participant architects and those listed below have our sincerest gratitude. We thank B. J. Archer; David Burres; Priscilla Cunningham; Diana Edkins, Permissions Editor, the Condé Nast Publications Inc., New York; Karen Wheeler of Michael Graves, Architect; Barbara Jakobson; James H. Jorgenson of Allan Greenberg, Architect; Ann Hoffman, Carolyn Hufbauer and Hugh Newell Jacobsen of the firm of the same name; R. Scott Johnson of Johnson/Burgee Architects; Glenn W. Arbonies, Emay Buck, James C. Childress, Mark Simon, all of Moore Grover Harper, Essex, Connecticut; Stephen Harby of Moore, Ruble, Yudell, Los Angeles; Carolyn Hackett of Kliment & Halsband; Arthur Drexler, Director of Architecture & Design, and Marie-Anne Evans, Assistant to Mr. Drexler, at the Museum of Modern Art; Suzanne Delehanty, Director, Neuberger Museum, Purchase, New York; Tyler Donaldson of James Stewart Polshek; Frances Nelson, Architecture Director of the Max Protetch Gallery; Stephen Estock of Venturi, Rauch and Scott Brown; Peter Pennoyer and Erica Millar of Robert A. M. Stern, Architects; Carolyn DeCato, Registrar, Martin Friedman, Director, Mildred Friedman, Curator of Design, of the Walker Art Center, Minneapolis, Minnesota. Finally, we thank David Brooke, Director of the Sterling and Francine Clark Art Institute, Williamstown, Massachusetts, and his staff for their aid in extending the life of the exhibition.

Only those who continually try to create, produce or disseminate information in the arts will know the gratitude individuals in institutions feel toward those donors who make such work possible. The long history of support at the Smith College Museum of Art is that of single individuals who demonstrate their approval of our activity through their gifts. To such people as Mrs. William A. Evans, Jr. (Charlotte Cushman '29), Philip Johnson, Mrs. James E.

Pollak (Mabel S. Brown '27), Mrs. T. V. Searing, Mr. and Mrs. Morton I. Sosland (Estelle Glatt '46), Mrs. Alfred R. Stern (Joanne Melniker '44), Enid Silver Winslow '54, mere words are not adequate thanks for their help. In recent years, a growing number of Museum Members have, through their regular donations and memberships, joined in the generosity of these individual donors. Sincere thanks as well are extended to Knoll International Inc. of New York City for its support. Most recently, the National Endowment for the Arts through the support of such exhibitions as this has provided the impetus for organizations of all sizes throughout the country to stretch themselves, to aspire to levels of quality heretofore not imagined. Their backing has been a rallying point for museums and their supporters. No one should be unaware that this support helps to enrich the quality of life of the whole nation.

Charles Chetham
Director

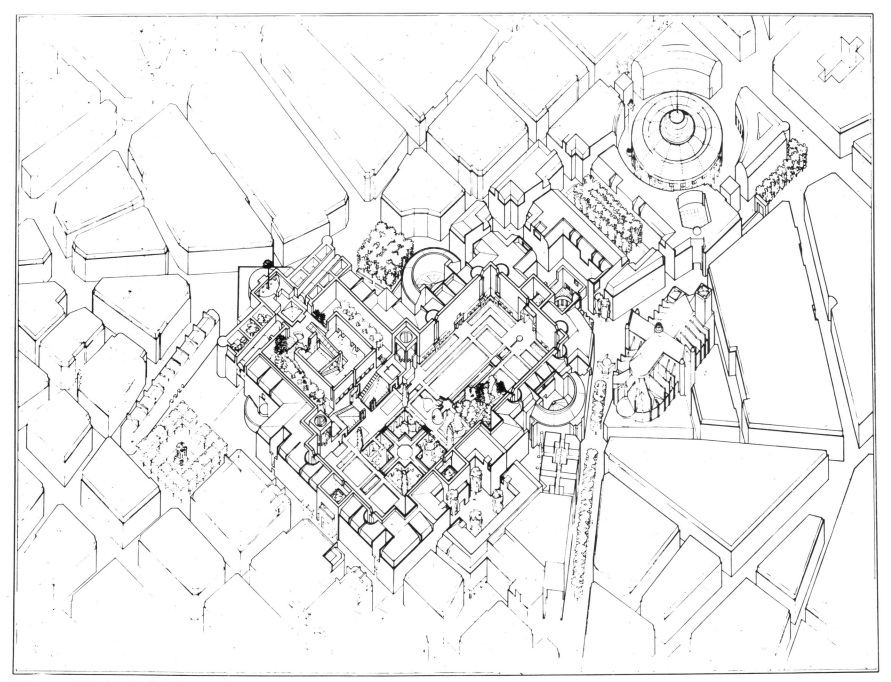

2. Peterson and Littenberg, *Les Halles Quarter*, 1979, cat. 100.

SPEAKING A NEW CLASSICISM: AMERICAN ARCHITECTURE NOW

Amid the Babel of architectural tongues clangoring around us today, some voices speaking a common language, albeit with many different accents, can be heard. For an increasing number of architects, the return to a classical language[1] offers an alternative to the unsettling polyglotism that has made recent professional practice and pedagogy so challenging and at times so frustrating. The new classicism represents a promising direction for American architecture in the 1980s, one that makes consensus possible while acknowledging the pluralistic promptings of our present society.

The words "classical" and "classicism" are used here not in the Apollonian sense of rationality, harmony, and measure, but in the literal sense denoting an ultimate, though not necessarily direct, origin in antiquity. With Sir John Summerson, we answer *no* when asked, "Is it possible . . . for a building to display absolutely none of the trappings associated with classical architecture and still, by virtue of proportion alone, to qualify as 'classical'? Classical architecture is only recognizable as such when it contains some allusion, however slight, however vestigial, to the orders."[2] Thus, by the "new classicism" we mean the presence in a given design of recognizably classical motifs (the orders, the aedicule), formats (the prostyle temple, the domed rotunda), and typologies (the Palladian villa, fig. 3; the Roman *castra*. However, this presence may be in the form of direct quotation or indirect allusion, the motifs may be whole or fragmented, the formats may be faithfully reproduced or tantalizingly inverted. Classical elements may be used structurally or decoratively, proportioned according to traditional or radically novel canons. Both pure and hybrid strains are cultivated, and irony and reverence contend.

The phenomenon singled out for examination in this exhibition might be regarded as being only part of that broader, still controversial movement in favor of "contextualism, allusionism, and ornamentalism."[3] After all, not all of the participants have been monogamously classicizing but some have flirted with other historical styles (among which *early* modernism must now be counted).

Nevertheless it seems worthwhile to consider the new classicism as a distinct manifestation, one which has had the most widespread application within the general retrieval of "The Presence of the Past,"[4] and the one with the greatest potential for the future. Charles Jencks's monograph, *Post-Modern Classicism: The New Synthesis,*[5] which appeared while this show was in preparation, gives support to our premise and serves as a valuable accompaniment to the exhibition.

But the net we have cast is of a different shape and texture. We have included architects who do not consider themselves *post*-modernists, and who rejected the term as prematurely coined and minted.[6] At the same time Jencks, demonstrating that a nostalgia for the classical syntax is international, illustrates projects from Asia, the Near East, and Europe, while we have confined our survey to the United States. We believe that a deliberate focusing on American examples is an essential first step to understanding the genesis and implications of the new classicism, and that the American contribution promises that maximum flexibility of grammar so desirable under the present circumstances. Historically, American interpretations of classicism have encompassed vernacular as well as more grandiloquent and academic idioms. Since colonial times, classicizing styles in this country have been directed toward both public and private realms, and have deftly accommodated regional peculiarities and a growing variety of building types and technologies. American classicism has been, and continues to be, characterized by pragmatism, good-natured wit, and generosity, characteristics which distinguish the projects in this exhibition from the tragic and politically charged visions of an Aldo Rossi or a Leon Krier,[7] who can scarcely be imagined concerning themselves with a single-family solar house (fig. 36, cat. 83–91), a suburban office building (cat. 43) or a loft renovation (fig. 37, cat. 92–95). While some of the participants, like Michael Graves, Philip Johnson, Rodolfo Machado and Jorge Silvetti, have been stimulated directly by monumental European models, nevertheless, like Benjamin Lat-

3. Palladio, *Villa Rotunda*, ca. 1550.

4. Blatteau, *Mount Pleasant*, 1976.

robe and Ithiel Town before them, they have been willing to adapt their solutions to local conditions. Others, like Robert Venturi, Charles Moore, and Robert Stern, are more eclectic at the outset, and have found as much inspiration in the work of Thomas Jefferson, Charles Follen McKim, and Colonial Williamsburg, as in Andrea Palladio, Karl Friedrich Schinkel (fig. 6), and Rome.

It is true that among the group of architects whose work appears in the exhibition—a group, incidentally, which spans several generations—no authoritative pattern of classical speech has yet emerged. As Edward Levin engagingly noted in a letter to the curator "mumbling or stammering the new classicism" might be a more appropriate title for the exhibition. Still, three generalizations might be hazarded. First, all of the projects represent a revolt against the monosyllabic, if not mute, stance of recent modernist architecture. At the same time, and this is the second point, each individual's diction has inevitably been influenced by the modernist assumptions that have dominated architectural practice for the last sixty years, differing mainly according to whether these assumptions have provoked reaction, revision, or a new synthesis. Finally, one period—that between 1750 and 1830—has provided the major formal sources. The architectural style of this era has been variously called "Romantic Classicism" ("the marriage of Faustus and Helen," as Walter Pater so felicitously put it, the wedding of Dionysian *Sturm and Drang* with Enlightenment Rationalism), "Revolutionary Classicism" (architectural style and content reflecting the intellectual, political, economic, and technological revolutions of the dawning industrial age), and, more neutrally, "Neo-Classicism."[8]

Several reasons may be advanced for the particular favor which this period enjoys at the present time. Knowledge of classical architecture had expanded exponentially following the important archaeological investigations which commenced in the 1730s, and the associated publications which illustrated with growing accuracy buildings from the furthest outposts of the ancient world.[9] Neo-Classical architects, therefore, had an increasingly large body of material to draw upon and, through their inclusive emulation of many different ancient, Renaissance and Mannerist models, they greatly enriched the repertoire of classicism. Furthermore, they used these models inventively, employing those devices of abstraction, fragmentation and inversion which appeal so much to today's audience shaped by modernism. Equally congenial to the current climate is the conception of *architecture parlante* (architecture which speaks) which was prevalent during that epoch.[10] Apparently disparate goals were also reconciled in many of the works produced during this period, when a love of picturesque nature was not incompatible with an admiration for geometrically-based architectural configurations.

Despite some broad similarities, no commonly accepted model of classical discourse has yet emerged among the architects in our exhibition. A few, like John Blatteau (cat. 3–8) and Allan Greenberg (fig. 45, cat. 29–35), present an historically consistent image in a given building, others offer a palimpsest of references which overlie and sometimes comment on one another. Blatteau's work is dependent on the academic tradition as it evolved in late eighteenth and nineteenth-century France and during the American Renaissance.[11] His project for Mount Pleasant House (fig. 4; not in exhibition) derives from Parisian architecture of the last third of the eighteenth century, while the Holy Redeemer hospital addition (fig. 27, cat. 9–12) is Beaux-Arts in spirit. Greenberg is more attracted by the classicism of the Federal period, which he considers the only classicism valid today, one "that goes back through Jefferson and Latrobe to Italy and ancient Rome. Most current architects look to the French eighteenth century, but after Gabriel's Petit Trianon, you can't go anywhere."[12]

More layered allusions are preferred by others. For his American Standard Home (cat. 57–62), Levin has incorporated a motif from Pavilion IX at the University of Virginia (fig. 5); Jefferson himself, lover of French Revolutionary architecture as well as of antiquity, had borrowed the apsidal recess screened by two columns from Claude-Nicolas Ledoux's Guimard House (fig. 6), so there is a double reference here. Still other echoes resound, perhaps fortuitously but meaningfully nonetheless. While Ledoux and Jefferson applied this motif to a façade, Robert Adam had used it for the interiors of his magnificent country houses, such as Syon House (figs. 7 and 8), and in so doing looked back directly, and through Palladio, to ancient Rome *thermae* (fig. 9). Finally, the plan (fig. 10) and certain interior features of the Standard Home stir recollections of Le Corbusier's Villa Savoye (fig. 11), often considered a twentieth-century descendant of the Palladian villa (fig. 3).[13] All these associations appear whole to the memory as a succession of after-images projected onto the new artifact, compelling conceptual and experiential comparisons. A more literal collage emerges in the work of Graves, who is less specific and complete in his references. In Cubist fashion he assembles fragments which, changed in scale and function and placed in unexpected contexts, acquire new and potent meanings. Graves's recent projects have a hauntingly poignant quality, like a poem whose verses we can only dimly recall.

This widely-accepted strategy of multiple, sometimes contradic-

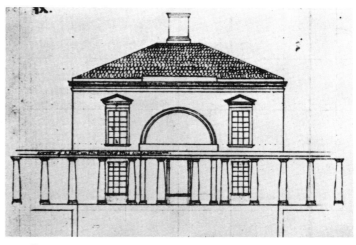

5. Jefferson, *Design for Pavilion IX, University of Virginia,* 1817–26.

6. Ledoux, *Design for Hôtel Guimard,* 1772.

7. Adam, *Syon House*, state dining room, 1761 and following.

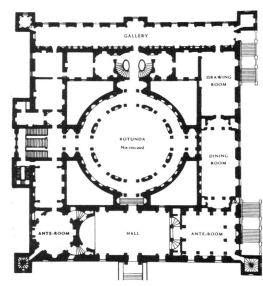

8. Adam, *Syon House*, plan, 1761 and following.

tory, allusionism, accords well with the modernist penchant for complexity, duality, and ambiguity. The Country House (fig. 47, cat. 45–49), by Robert Kliment and Frances Halsband, was based, at the client's request, on the Georgian Wythe House in Colonial Williamsburg, itself a combination of eighteenth- and twentieth-century inclinations. The elegant simplicity of the detailing and the composition of the garden front, however, also recall Josef Hoffmann's Palais Stoclet (fig. 12) in Brussels. Hoffmann and other Viennese Secessionists produced an Austrian variant of the Art Nouveau that derived its inspiration not directly from nature but via the Hellenic idealization of natural forms; this Viennese version, unlike many other manifestations of the *fin-de-siècle,* survived to become an important link with Art Deco classicism. Robert Stern, in his competition entry for the DOM Hardware Company Headquarters (fig. 40, cat. 116–20) in Germany, also looks to early twentieth-century Vienna, paying homage to Otto Wagner in his choice and articulation of materials, and in the lucid geometries of the massing, though the latter evokes Neo-Classical reminiscences as well. His project for Llewellyn Park (cat. 121–24) summons yet other shades. Given the sympathetic task of renovating a Neo-Georgian house designed in 1929 by Edgar Williams, Stern found himself working with an historical object that recalled both colonial times and the Jazz Age. The latter association is reinforced by the Art Deco tile patterns in the pool house addition, but they supply only one ingredient in this curious, if not contrary, mélange of grotto and greenhouse, of primitivism and high tech, of brutality and elegance. The heavy rustication and the archaic proportions of the Doric columns are derived from the works of Romantic Classicists like Ledoux, who sought to mirror the sublimity of nature in architectural forms of crude strength and elemental power. An additional late eighteenth-century conceit—"sunken architecture"—is used to affirm the connection between building and landscape: Stern half buries the pool house in the hillside. On the interior the link with nature is maintained via the palm tree columns. These imitate John Nash's at the Royal Pavilion in Brighton, but simultaneously they suggest the arboreal origin of the column, and this in turn leads us to the Abbé Laugier.

Laugier's *Essai sur l'Architecture* appeared in 1753. In this influential treatise, he argued that the rustic hut (fig. 13), man's presumed first dwelling, provides the archetype for all subsequent architectural evolution.[14] His primitive dwelling, in which naturalism of materials coexists with rationalism of organization, captured the fancy of his own contemporaries, and subsequently of some of ours. Thus the primitive hut, as interpreted by the Danish Romantic Classicist, C. F. Hansen (fig. 14), becomes the gazebo of Graves's house in Aspen (fig. 30, cat. 18–21). In other incarnations it crowns his Red River Heritage Center (fig. 31, cat. 22–28) and his Portland Office building (fig. 15; not in exhibition). Graves resurrects the primitive hut to make us aware of the necessary interdependence of the buildings we construct and the natural world.[15] His preoccupation with this archetypal structure is understandable, given his methods and intentions. Alan Colquhoun has cogently observed of Graves that he employs the language of Cubism and of the classical tradition:

> to recreate an architecture out of its primordial elements; to offer a new and intense interpretation of architecture itself and of man's cultural predicament in relation to nature. . . . His work contains a continual dialectic between architecture as the product of reason, setting itself against nature, and architecture as a metaphor for nature.[16]

Such an awareness of context, built as well as natural, was conspicuously lacking among the masters of the Modern Movement, but it has become an important issue for the architects in this exhibition. It has been essential for the two architectural firms—Machado and Silvetti, and Peterson and Littenberg—represented by impressive urban projects requiring the transformation of a large area of a city, without destroying the existing matrix, in the case of the Steps of Providence (fig. 34, cat. 63–72), or the contiguous fabric, in the case of the quarter of Les Halles (fig. 2, cat. 96–101). Contextualism has also impinged on the design decisions of Peter Gluck and James Polshek, whose allegiance to certain values of modernism is more firm, and whose interest in classicism is less exacting, than many others included here. Their residences display what they describe as a "conscious schizophrenia" (in the currently fashionable semiological terminology this would be called "double-coding"). In one façade, classical elements are subtly incorporated; in the other, the vocabulary of the International Style persists. New England traditions have been acknowledged by Gluck in the front half of his house in Lincoln, Massachusetts. The prior existence of older. classicizing buildings on Polshek's and Gluck's Delafield Estate (fig. 38, cat. 102–6) similarly suggested formal choices of a kind which make that project wholly compatible with the theme of the new classicism. One might note at this point that the International Style itself had a hidden classical agenda;[17] however, the overt classical allusionism of the present time is in fact directed against that merely syntactical (compositional), as opposed to rhetorical (expressive), use of classicism.[18]

The wide range of single and superimposed classical associations

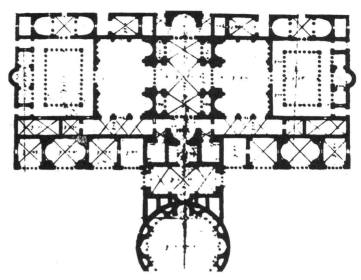

9. Palladio, *Reconstruction, Baths of Agrippa.*

10. Levin, *American Standard Home,* plan, 1979.

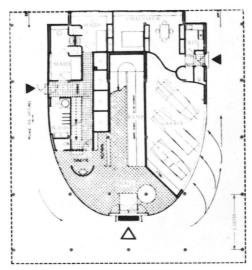

11. Le Corbusier, *Villa Savoye,* plan, 1929–30.

12. Hoffmann, *Palais Stoclet,* garden façade, 1905–11.

identified above has been achieved by an assortment of design tactics. Scale distortion is a common device, as is reversal of solid and void, of opacity and transparency. In the country house by Robert Harper with Charles Moore (fig. 46, cat. 36–42), glass has replaced fluted stone in the "pilasters" which frame the pavilions, just as the "ribs" of the living-room "dome" (which is suspended rather than supported from below) are in fact the open spaces between the segments (fig. 17). In Stern's Forum Design Pavilion (fig. 16; not in exhibition) in Linz, the archaic Doric column is in fact a void generated by the downward-tapering piers which lie beneath the over-scaled triglyphs. A somewhat similar ploy stimulates the psyche when Richard Oliver apparently bifurcates a wall in the Pittman Loft (fig. 37, cat. 92–95) in New York City. The moldings complete the circuit on the outer edges, turning the corner in correct fashion, but on the inner face are left exposed (fig. 18), demonstrating on the one hand how they were put together, but on the other creating a sense of tension, for the viewer wants to join together what seems to have been rent asunder. This projection of parts of a once unified whole into separate fields can be seen in Venturi's country house (figs. 42–44), cat. 131–34), where the pilasters have been displaced from the façade to form a portico. More complicated Cubist strategies are employed by Graves, who may disassemble an architectural entity, like a façade or a portal, into its constituent parts and recompose these so that they are no longer contiguous. A keystone may be removed from its expected position (resulting in that inversion of solid and void noted previously) so that it can reappear at a distance, in the customary vertical plane or, horizontally, in plan. That simultaneity of viewpoint sought by Cubist artists is hereby achieved, as is a more resonant union of interior and exterior, building and site.

The substitution of contemporary materials for traditional ones is another device that produces novel configurations. Moore's Piazza d'Italia (fig. 19) in New Orleans has column capitals of chromium and moldings of neon. Blatteau's wall for the Bayonne Hospital (cat. 3) is not constructed of bricks and mortar but cast in large pieces. For the Knoll International Showroom (fig. 20, cat. 135–37) in New York City, Venturi translated into painted glass the stucco ceiling of Robert Adam's Etruscan Room at Osterley Park, and low relief arabesques were transformed into linear patterns. But traditional materials like wood and plaster continue to be used as well. Although twentieth-century practices in the building trades do not encourage lavish ornament, the new classicism gives the lie to the dogma that decoration is economically and technically impossible (if not immoral[19]) in an industrialized age. Oliver (fig. 18) and Moore have found ready-made wooden pieces in the lumberyard which could be assembled to make simple classical moldings, while some of the classicizing details which Johnson ordered from builders' catalogues for his Sugarland office building cost far less than the high-tech items more usually specified. Furthermore there will always be architects who know how to design beautiful ornamental details (fig. 21) and craftsmen who know how to make them. Relegated for most of the twentieth century to the patronage of the patronized interior decorator, such skilled artisans now discover that architects are eager to employ their talents once more.

The dimensions of personal choice permitted by the new classicism can be demonstrated by examining alternative interpretations of the same residential typology. Mount Vernon (fig. 22) was the starting point for both Greenberg and Venturi in their country-house projects, but Greenberg has "corrected" the artisan dissonances of the original while Venturi has exaggerated them. Greenberg's training and his faithful study of classicizing architects like Sir Edwin Lutyens[20] have encouraged him to create a knowing version informed by those qualities of serenity, resolution and grandeur associated for centuries with the classical tradition. In contrast Venturi, whose attraction to Mannerism has been an inspiration since the beginning of his independent practice,[21] performs a different operation on the dream house of the father of our country. While the entrance façade of the original is not strictly symmetrical, at least the door is in the center. Venturi also establishes a central axis via the pediment, but then shoves the entrance as well as the windows vigorously aside. The modernist shibboleths of the *plan générateur* and of asymmetricality are ironically honored here within a framework that revokes them. Venturi's call for "both/and" rather than "either/or," and his interest in duality, inflection and accommodation (the front door inflects to accommodate the stair) are reflected here. The naughty behavior of the pilasters (transformed from George Washington's piers) on the rear façade has already been remarked; here too we have "both/and," since visually they share the same plane as the doors and shutters.

The American Greek Revival house is another typology that has recently intrigued architects. In his New England House of 1979 (figs. 24 and 25; not in exhibition), Hugh Newell Jacobsen has accommodated the various spaces required in a domestic program to the rather rigid format of the temple by using three aedicular pavilions placed parallel to one another and joined by service wings. A sort of mini-Acropolis reminiscent of many examples of American domestic and collegiate architecture, like T. U. Walter's Girard College in Philadelphia, is the result. More commonly, the smaller

13. *The Primitive Hut*, frontispiece, Marc-Antoine Laugier, *Essai sur l'Architecture*, 1753, engraved by Ch. Eisen.

14. Graves, *House in Aspen*, gazebo studies, 1978.

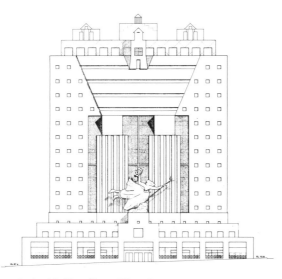

15. Graves, *Portland Public Office Building,* Oregon, 1980.

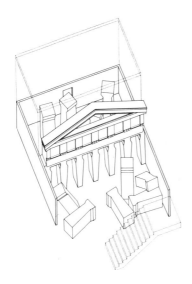

16. Stern, *Forum Design Pavilion,* Linz, Austria, 1980.

"temples" were set at right angles to the main one. This solution received a beautiful execution in the Bowers House (fig. 23) by Ithiel Town, that once graced Northampton's Prospect Street, and it has also been adapted by Levin for his Solar House (fig. 26, cat. 54–56). The more correct tetrastyle portico has been reduced, as so often occurred during the heyday of the Greek Revival, resulting in the provincial anomaly of a central axis marked by a column rather than a doorway. The ingenuity characteristic of much vernacular Greek Revival architecture has been sustained here, in the contrasting configuration of the wings and in the double-functioning "columns" which, filled with water, are part of the solar energy equipment, as they are also in the solar house designed by Christopher and Timothy Morris (fig. 36, cat. 83–91).

The reflections on the new classicism summarized above suggest only a few of the relevant issues raised by this movement. Others can be mentioned only briefly. For example, methods of architectural representation have had to respond to the new—and in some cases, old—architectural criteria accompanying the new classicism. Novel techniques of drafting have been invented and conventional ones revived, as the drawings in this exhibition demonstrate.[22] The spare line drawings, often mere notations, which were standard fare until recently, are inadequate to the demands for polychromy and ornament. Nor can architects trained to render only schematically cope graphically with the recovery of the wall as the prime determinant of architectural form. For most of the twentieth century, space (universal and fluid) and rationalized structure have been considered the only important architectural concerns. Now the enclosing membrane again takes on weight, mass, figurative content, to create tangible boundaries which mark place and set up hierarchies of movement and activity.[23]

Signs and portents during the last twenty-five or thirty years which forecast the new classicism abound. In tracing the genealogy of this movement, the careers of three architects in particular merit careful notice—Eero Saarinen, Louis I. Kahn, and most of all Philip Johnson. The burgeoning popular support for historical preservation has obviously contributed to the growth of the new classicism. The public has been forced to examine and evaluate older structures, many of which belong to the classical tradition, and architects have been forced to learn, or relearn, the classical vocabulary. The admiring wonder that the orders consistently arouse seems never to have died. Untiring defenders of the classical tradition in America who never abandoned hope of its recovery, like Henry Hope Reed, have helped to ease the transition from modernist exclusivity and antihistoricism.

Serious architectural literature devoted to classicism has proliferated. The explosion of interest in Romantic Classicism has been documented in note 8; one should also cite modern studies of sixteenth-century architecture, especially Rudolph Wittkower's *Architectural Principles in the Age of Humanism*.[24] More recently there has been renewed appreciation for the Beaux-Arts Classicism of France and the United States, sparked by the Museum of Modern Art's exhibition of 1975 and the accompanying catalogue.[25] When one considers that the International Style was launched to an overwhelming success in this country by the same museum's exhibition of 1932,[26] the controversial reverberations occasioned by the later show can be understood.

The renewed interest in architectural history in colleges and graduate schools has also played a role in shaping the phenomenon under review. The *Prix de Rome* and the traveling fellowships which allow examination of historical architecture at first hand are eagerly sought by the most gifted students. Many of the most visible architectural historians, like Henry-Russell Hitchcock, Vincent Scully, William L. MacDonald, James Ackerman, Spiro Kostof, and Neil Levine, find a captivated audience among architects as well as the general public. All, significantly, have a scholarly commitment not only to twentieth-century architecture but to various classical periods as well.[27] Karen Vogel Wheeler, an associate in Michael Graves's office, remembers Professor MacDonald in 1968 telling her and her classmates at Smith College to "learn your columns—you are going to need to know them some day."

Voltaire's dictum about God might be applied with equal force to classicism. But classicism does exist; what is necessary is to *re*-invent it in every age to answer the programmatic and symbolic requirements of that age in ways responsive to the available building technologies and economic resources. In the 1980s, such a challenge awaits American architecture.

Helen Searing

Notes

[1] The best general introduction to the terminology and history of architectural classicism is Sir John Summerson, *The Classical Language of Architecture* (Cambridge: The MIT Press, 1976), which began life as a BBC broadcast in 1963. Here, Sir John uses "language" metaphorically, conveying that time-honored and straightforward understanding of architecture as an expressive as well as functional art; the late eighteenth-century term

17. Harper, *Country House*, interior dome, 1980–81, cat. 41.

18. Oliver, *Molding for the Pittman Loft*, 1979–80 (see cat. 95).

19. Moore, *Piazza d'Italia*, columns, 1978.

20. Venturi, *Knoll International*, 1979–80, cat. 135.

architecture parlante (see note 10 below) connotes the same idea. Within the last twenty years, however, in linguistic and semiological circles, a more sophisticated and abstruse theoretical debate has developed in which "language" is used analogically. Linguistic structure is here regarded as the archetypal form of communication and architectural parallels with phonemes, syntagms, *langue, parole, écriture,* and deep syntactical structure are relentlessly pursued. A third approach is taken by Christian Norberg-Schulz, who derives his interpretation from the ontology of Martin Heidegger: "The language of architecture expresses the existential structure called 'Spatiality'. . . . Together, topology, morphology, and typology make up the language of architecture" [Norberg-Schulz, "Kahn, Heidegger, and the Language of Architecture," *Oppositions* 18 (Fall, 1979), pp. 41–44]. Our use of linguistic terms in this essay is metaphorical, as we believe that the investigations referred to above have tended to place too heavy a philosophical burden on architecture, removing us too far from the traditional sensual, emotional, and cerebral joys of architectural experience. Nonetheless linguistic analyses are fascinating and often illuminating and the interested reader is referred to the following: Mario Gandelsonas, "From Structure to Subject: The Formation of an Architectural Language," *Oppositions* 17 (Summer, 1979), pp. 6–29; Ivor Indyk, "Literary Theory and Architectural Practice," *International Architect* I, no. 1 (1979), pp. 52–53; Jacques Guillerme, "The Idea of Architectural Language: A Critical Inquiry," *Oppositions* 10 (Fall, 1977), pp. 21–26; Jorge Silvetti, "The Beauty of Shadows," *Oppositions* 9 (Summer, 1977), pp. 43–61. For a popular treatment of the linguistic analogy see Charles Jencks, *The Language of Post-Modern Architecture* (revised enlarged edition, New York: Rizzoli International, 1977), and for a history of earlier applications, see Peter Collins, *Changing Ideals in Modern Architecture* (Montreal: McGill University Press, 1967), chapter on "The Linguistic Analogy." *Meaning in Architecture,* edited by Charles Jencks and George Baird (New York: George Braziller, 1969) offers a collection of essays dealing with the semiological dimensions of architecture.

2 Summerson, *op. cit.,* p. 8. For that reason we do not include architects like Peter Eisenman or John Hejduk, whose designs are sometimes compared schematically to Palladian villas. Arguably, the Roosevelt Island project by Mario Gandelsonas and Diana Agrest might have been appropriate, since they suggest that we "read" the rounded glass towers as "fragments of a Greek temple designed in a colossal order" (*International Architect* I, no. 1, p. 51). However, without their suggestion, it is unlikely that such a reading would occur.

3 Robert A. M. Stern's three constituents of Post-Modernism [see his *New Directions in American Architecture* (revised edition, New York: George Braziller, 1979), pp. 127–33]. Most of those who used the term "post-modern" would agree that these are the most important components.

4 The title of the 1980 Venice *Biennale*'s architecture section and of the accompanying catalogue (English edition, New York: Rizzoli International, 1980). A number of the architects represented in the Smith

College exhibition participated in this *Biennale.*

5 *Post-Modern Classicism* (London: Architectural Design and Academy Editions, 1980) contains important statements from the architects in addition to the useful introduction by Jencks.

6 This is not the place to enter that particular fray. Interested readers will find a plethora of commentary in the professional and popular press. A series of relevant articles can be found in *The Harvard Architecture Review I: Beyond the Modern Movement* (Cambridge: The MIT Press, Spring, 1980), among which are contributions from Jorge Silvetti, Denise Scott Brown and Robert Venturi, Robert Stern, Steven Peterson, and Stanley Tigerman. Another publication that can be recommended is the second volume of *Precis* (New York: Columbia University Graduate School of Architecture and Planning, 1980), dedicated to "Tradition: Radical and Conservative." *Oppositions,* the organ of the Institute for Architecture and Urban Studies in New York, published and distributed by the MIT Press, is also required reading on this issue. For a critic's view, see Ada Louis Huxtable, "The Troubled State of Modern Architecture," *Architectural Record* 169, no. 1 (January, 1981), pp. 72–79; the same article appeared in *The New York Review of Books* XXVII, no. 7 (May 1, 1980), pp. 22–23, 26–29.

7 For Rossi, see F. Moschini, editor, *Aldo Rossi: Projects and Drawings 1962–1979* (New York: Rizzoli International, 1979); for Krier, see Leon Krier, *Architectural Drawings for the Reconstruction of the European City* (Brussels: Archives d'Architecture Moderne, 1980). See also *Rational Architecture Rationnelle* (Brussels: Archives d'Architecture Moderne, 1978), and Charles Jencks, "Irrational Rationalism," in *The Rationalists,* edited by D. Sharp (London: The Architectural Press), as well as the catalogue cited in note 4.

8 The modern study of late eighteenth-century classicism begins in Germany in the 1920s; for these early German publications by such historians as Sigfried Giedion and Emil Kaufmann, see the article by Teyssot cited at the end of this note. Milestones in English include Kaufmann, "Three Revolutionary Architects: Boullée, Ledoux, Lequeu," *Transactions of the American Philosophical Society,* nos. 42/43 (1952), pp. 431–564; Kaufmann, *Architecture in the Age of Reason* (Cambridge: Harvard University Press, 1954); the publications of Robin Middleton; Robert Rosenblum, *Transformations in Late Eighteenth-Century Art* (Princeton: Princeton University Press, 1967); Hugh Honour, *Neo-Classicism* (Harmondsworth: Penguin Books, 1968); *The Age of Neo-Classicism* (catalogue, London: Arts Council of Great Britain, 1972); J. Mordaunt Crook, *The Greek Revival* (London: John Murray, 1972); and Allan Braham, *The Architecture of the French Enlightenment* (Berkeley: University of California, 1980). Crook and Braham give useful discussions on the problems of nomenclature; the most thorough treatment of terminology will be found in Georges Teyssot, "Emil Kaufmann and the Architecture of Reason: Klassizismus and 'Revolutionary Architecture,'" *Oppositions* 13 (Summer, 1978), pp. 46–75.

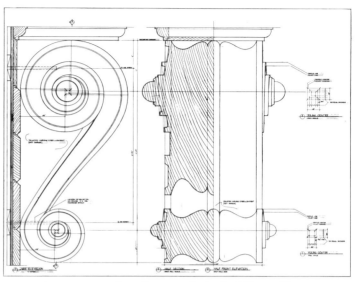

21. Greenberg, *Connecticut Farm House,* console detail, 1979, cat. 33.

22. *Mount Vernon.* Courtesy of the Mount Vernon Ladies Association.

[9] For an exhaustive survey of eighteenth-century architectural and archaeological publications, see Appendix A in Carroll L. V. Meeks, *Italian Architecture 1750–1914* (New Haven: Yale University Press, 1966).

[10] The idea that architecture is a communicative as well as a functional art was well understood by the later eighteenth century and was related to the concept of associationism [see George Hersey, *High Victorian Gothic: A Study in Associationism* (Baltimore: Johns Hopkins University Press, 1972)]. This concept was extended to include ethical implications by Gothic Revivalists like Pugin and Ruskin [see David Watkin, *Morality and Architecture* (Oxford: Clarendon Press, 1971)], and became an important component of modernist theory.

[11] By American Renaissance we refer to the classical eclecticism which dominated American architecture from the 1880s through the 1920s, when eighteenth-century colonial styles (e.g., Georgian) were revived for domestic and collegiate architecture, and ancient and Renaissance Roman forms were used for more monumental urban programs. The rubric covers the work of men like McKim, Cass Gilbert, Daniel H. Burnham, Ernest Flagg, Henry Bacon, and John Russell Pope, and firms like Carrère and Hastings, Warren and Wetmore, Clinton and Russell, Delano and Aldrich, and Bakewell and Brown, to name a few. For a fascinating contemporary view, when European modernism was just making inroads against the American Renaissance, see G. H. Edgell, *The American Architecture of Today* (New York: Charles Scribner's Sons, 1928). A more recent compendium is Walter S. Kidney, *The Architecture of Choice: Eclecticism in America* (New York: George Braziller, 1974). Joy Dow, *American Renaissance* (New York, William T. Comstock, 1904), does *not* use this term in the accepted sense but presents a history of American domestic architecture from the colonial times to 1900. The publications of Henry Hope Reed, and of the organization Classical America (among whose officers are Reed, Blatteau, and Greenberg) have been important in keeping alive this version of classicism (see Mr. Reed's essay in this catalogue).

[12] Conversation with Allan Greenberg, July, 1980.

[13] See, for example, Colin Rowe, "The Mathematics of the Ideal Villa: Palladio and Le Corbusier Compared," *The Architectural Review* 101, no. 603 (March, 1947), pp. 101–10; Rowe is at some pains, however, to emphasize fundamental differences as well. John Jacobus, *Twentieth-Century Architecture 1940–65* (London: Thames and Hudson, 1966) also refers to Palladio in connection with Le Corbusier, and to the "latent and secret Hellenism" of the Villa Savoye (p. 22).

[14] For Laugier, see Wolfgang Herrmann, *Laugier and Eighteenth-Century French Theory* (London: A. Zwemmer, 1962); Laugier's *Essai* itself has been reprinted in a modern facsimile (Farnborough: Gregg Press Ltd., 1966). See also Anthony Vidler, "The Third Typology," *Rational Architecture Rationelle,* pp. 28–32.

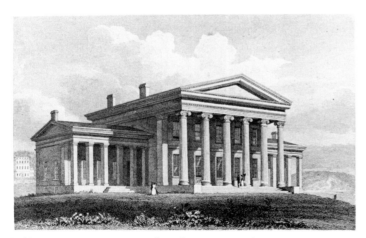

23. Town, *Bowers House,* ca. 1827, drawn by Alexander Jackson Davis, engraved by Fenner Sears & Co. Courtesy of Forbes Library, Northampton, Massachusetts.

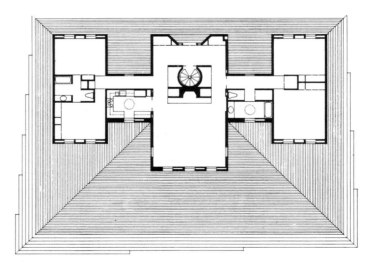

24. Jacobsen, *New England House,* view, 1979.

15 For Graves, the primitive hut seems to symbolize the profane domain of the Noble Savage in his rustic hut and garden, as against the sacred domain of Adam in Paradise; Graves feels that modern man has not been able to choose between these two realms. See his comments on the Aspen house, in *International Architect* I, no. 1, pp. 13–25.

16 Alan Colquhoun in *Michael Graves* (New York: Rizzoli International, 1979), p. 17. A modified version of this article, "From Bricolage to Myth," appears in *Oppositions* 12 (Spring, 1978).

17 Philip Johnson, in his monograph *Mies van der Rohe* (New York: Museum of Modern Art, 1947), discussed the Neo-Classical roots of Mies and the importance to him of Schinkel. Colin Rowe's writings, especially the article cited in note 13, and "Mannerism in Modern Architecture," *The Architectural Review* 107, no. 641 (May, 1950), pp. 289–99, provide valuable insights into this relationship. See also Reyner Banham's entry "Neoclassicism," in *Encyclopedia of Modern Architecture*, edited by Gerd Hatje (London: Thames and Hudson, 1963). Many of the pioneers of modern architecture were thorough-going classicists at some point in their careers, among them Otto Wagner, Peter Behrens, Auguste Perret, Tony Garnier, and Adolf Loos.

18 Robert A. M. Stern, "Classicism in Context," *Post-Modern Classicism*, pp. 38–39.

19 A constant association made by many modernists was that of ornament with bourgeois extravagance, conspicuous consumption, and snobbery. Because many of those same modernists professed leftist politics, any-thing that smacked of the middle-class was anathema. Ornament also fell victim to the mechanidolatry of early twentieth-century theorists and designers. Adolf Loos's equation of Ornament and Crime [see Reyner Banham, *Theory and Design in the First Machine Age* (London: The Architectural Press, 1960)] was the most extreme and therefore the best known tirade, though Loos himself was devoted to classical ornament.

20 Allan Greenberg prepared the exhibition on Lutyens (a great Edwardian architect whose rather Mannerist spatial plays have made him a favorite among architects like Venturi and Stern as well as Greenberg), held at the Museum of Modern Art in 1978. His article "Lutyens' Architecture Restudied" is published in *Perspecta* 12 (1970).

21 Venturi's appreciation of Mannerism is made clear in his first book, *Complexity and Contradiction in Architecture* (New York: Museum of Modern Art, 1966), a publication which, more than any other single work cited in these notes, turned architecture in the direction under review.

22 See Robert A. M. Stern, "Architecture Now: Drawing Towards a More Modern Architecture," *Architectural Design* 47, no. 6 (June, 1977).

23 See for example Steven Peterson, "Space and Anti-Space," *The Harvard Architecture Review I*, pp. 89–113. Michael Graves has concerned himself very much with this issue.

25. Jacobsen, *New England House*, plan, 1979.

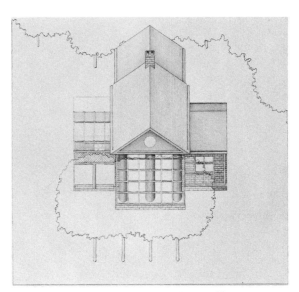

26. Levin, *A Solar Greek-Revival House*, 1980–81, cat. 55.

[24] First published as three articles in the *Journal of the Warburg and Courtauld Institutes,* 1940 to 1945. See Henry A. Millon, "Rudolf Wittkower, Architectural Principles in the Age of Humanism: Its Influence on the Development and Interpretation of Modern Architecture," *Journal of the Society of Architectural Historians* 31, no. 2 (May, 1972), pp. 83–91.

[25] Arthur Drexler, editor, *The Architecture of the Ecole des Beaux-Arts* (New York: Museum of Modern Art, 1977).

[26] In 1932 Alfred Barr, Henry-Russell Hitchcock, and Philip Johnson introduced European modernist architecture to the general public in the exhibition and catalogue, *Modern Architecture, International Exhibition* (New York: Museum of Modern Art, 1932); a companion volume by Hitchcock and Johnson, *The International Style: Architecture since 1922,* was published by W. W. Norton & Company the same year. The participation of Johnson is especially interesting, since he perhaps earlier and more than anyone has been responsible for the reaction against the International Style since the 1950s. See Philip Johnson, *Writings* (New York: Oxford University Press, 1979).

[27] Hitchcock, whom Smith College so proudly claims, was a visiting lecturer at Yale and Harvard and has been a professor emeritus at the Institute of Fine Arts in New York City; his indispensable compendium, *Architecture: Nineteenth and Twentieth Centuries* (third edition, Baltimore: Harmond Penguin Books, 1968) begins with Romantic Classicism; Scully, at Yale, has published on ancient Greek temples and their siting as well as on the late nineteenth-century colonial revival; MacDonald, who went from Yale to Smith, and has been visiting lecturer at a number of architectural schools, is a scholar on ancient and Baroque Roman architecture; James Ackerman, who went from Berkeley to Harvard, is a specialist on the Italian Renaissance; Spiro Kostof, now at Berkeley, has written on a wide range of classical monuments, including those of fascist Italy; and Neil Levine, at Harvard, has provided brilliant insights into nineteenth-century Neo-Grec architecture.

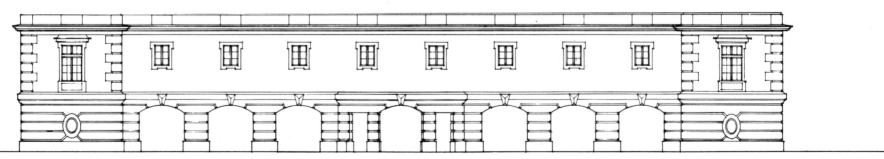

27. Blatteau, *Holy Redeemer Hospital,* 1981, cat. 10.

THE CLASSICAL TRADITION IN MODERN TIMES: A PERSONAL ASSESSMENT

What, it may be asked, is the classical tradition in art? The simplest definition, and it is that of the Washington artist Pierce Rice, is that it is an idealized and generalized interpretation of nature first initiated by the Greeks and the Romans and given fresh life in the Renaissance which began in Italy in the fifteenth century to lapse in America in the 1930s.

In painting and sculpture it is best seen in the treatment of the human form. The classical figure is a composite of a variety of models, that is, the work of the ancients and their followers and the live model. The classical artist does not need the live model in front of him as does the realist (naturalist), he depends on his knowledge, skill and imagination. In architecture, the classical is identified not by proportions, nor by plan, nor by materials, however important, but by ornament. All styles are identified by ornament, be they Arabic, Indian, Chinese or other, except the modern, the one style which has no ornament. (A current phrase among architectural critics is "stripped classical." This is an oxymoron because a building "stripped," i.e. stripped of ornament, is not classical.)

In mentioning artistic styles of other cultures we are reminded of the fact that the classical is the main artistic tradition of Western civilization. What is more, other minor Western styles such as the Gothic are derived from it or, as in the case of modern art, in rebellion against it. What distinguishes the tradition from all others is the importance given the human figure. We need only turn to America's greatest building, our National Capitol, to grasp at once the role which the human form occupies in the classical.

In fact, the National Capitol underscores the dimension of the tradition, not only in the presence of the human figure and its treatment, but also in the joining of the arts in one building, an example of interweaving unrivaled in the nation. From bronze work to stone carving they are, with few exceptions, found here.

Other than the human figure, identification is furnished by the acanthus leaf which, as the architect John Barrington Bayley has pointed out, is to Western art what the chrysanthemum is to Japanese art and the lotus to Egyptian.

What, then, occurred that the classical tradition should die in our time? Why did the West, above all other cultures, see fit to reject its heritage? It did not happen overnight. Professor Hans Sedlmayr of Salzburg sees the first signs of rebellion in certain aspects of the cult for the picturesque landscape in the eighteenth century. This would seem hard to believe of a fashion which sprang from the classical canvases of Poussin and Claude. Geoffrey Scott in his *Architecture of Humanism* is more specific. Where he sees the conflict is in the *picturesque ideal* which he finds "at variance with tradition and repugnant to design."

Instead of the picturesque landscape as the start of the break-away others, such as the mural decorator Kenyon Cox, find it in a shift in painting. Jacques-Louis David, according to Cox, was the first in modern times to reject the classical, the classical given a new dimension in the Renaissance by Raphael. The French painter and revolutionary opted for what was to become realism.

But of far greater influence was Romantic literature, especially Romantic literary criticism. The interest in nature, in the primitive, in the fragment and, most important of all, in the concept of originality comes from literature of the Romantic era. The cult of the fragment in poetry was in vogue before Rodin saw fit to introduce it into sculpture. One can say that the skilled modeller adopted the fragment in order to set himself apart, to be original, because so many in his day had forsaken the classical for the realistic figure but the figure treated whole.

The dominant note of our time is the aim of originality which, in the arts, first appeared in painting and sculpture. The object today is to be different at all costs. No longer is beauty the goal of the artist, only originality even if it takes the shape of ugliness, brutality and obscenity.

In architecture, unlike painting and sculpture, another instrument to attain originality came into being, namely so-called functionalism or, to use its nineteenth century label, rationalism. By wholly disregarding the lessons of the past except the structural (mechanical), by accepting only the basic requirements of a structure, the architect would achieve an original building. And what was more it would have the added virtue, as often boasted, of being "of our time." The theorist who linked the original and the functional was, of course, Viollet-le-Duc. The extraordinary Frenchman, the first theoretical preservationist, based his thesis on a mechanical interpretation of the Gothic and, in this way, set the theoretical foundation for the overthrow of the classical which took the name of modern architecture.

That the artist seeking originality inevitably fell into the trap of imitating his colleagues made no difference. The appeal remains unchanged as the word itself, much like the word, creative, has become part of everyday vocabulary. We read of "original research" today as often as we see a sign proclaiming "creative dry cleaning." Should the artist, fearing to be identified with anyone else, turn away from what his colleagues are doing he takes refuge, without theory, in plain ugliness

The seduction offered by the concept of originality was especially felt among critics, editors and journalists at a time when the press had become powerful. The "originals," especially if they shocked, could count on the favor of the media. In leafing through *Vanity Fair,* the most trendy of publications between the wars, the reader will find mention of Le Corbusier, Gropius and other European Secessionists but not a word of Arthur Brown, Jr., the classical architect of the San Francisco City Hall, any more than he will find mention of Philip Trammell Shutze of Atlanta. In those decades Lewis Mumford in his column of *The New Yorker* attacked the classical and promoted the modern.

Others were not immune. There is that category which might be best described as "middle-class rebels," persons who, more than customarily, reject the world of their parents. Such was the sponsorship of the Museum of Modern Art of New York which was founded for the sole purpose of educating Americans to like the modern. That institution was the most powerful single force in promoting the replacement of the traditional by the modern in the 1930s. (One of its devices was publishing; it was the largest publisher of art books around 1940.)

Nor should the social overtones of the modern message be overlooked. Le Corbusier had announced "Architecture or Revolution," his idea being that architecture would so shape society that there would be no purpose to revolution. High on the list of the modernists was the call for public housing. They dismissed the classical men as being architects of the rich and therefore wholly indiffer-

ent to the needs of the underprivileged. (That Ernest Flagg and others of the American Renaissance were concerned, and even designed housing which was built, was unknown to them, or they sought to disregard the work of the classical men.) Planning for the masses, part of what came to be called "total design," was another boasted aim of the new breed of architects, many of whom glowed with a megalomania which still afflicts the professions.

A cruel irony lay in the preoccupation of many modernists with the social ills of the day, especially in the 1930s. Evidently it never dawned on them that their bare style, wholly lacking in ornament, wholly divorced from the other arts, would virtually destroy the centuries-old crafts. (I can recall driving by the Museum of Modern Art, when its building on 53rd Street off Fifth Avenue was new, with employees of E. F. Caldwell and Company, one of the leading electric fixture and bronze working firms of the country. They turned angrily and shook their fists at the bare wall, shouting "That Goddamn place is destroying us. Those _____ are killing us." At the time I was surprised and bemused. Later I realized that they were only too justified in yelling. Caldwell, which employed a thousand bronzeurs, marble workers, model makers and designers, was only one of many craft firms which were to disappear.) As the old craftsmen died off, especially those doing architectural sculpture, the modern architect, when asked why he did not design a classical building, would smile in a superior way and say "I would be delighted to do it but where are the craftsmen?" This is a very sorry aspect of the triumph of the modern, one wholly neglected by our historians.

As originality raged through the arts leaving a trail of visual nihilism and destroying the ancient skills, a few traditionalists, a tiny minority, remained untouched. We think of Maxfield Parrish who stood apart and retained a faithful clientele to 1961 when he stopped painting at the age of ninety. The interior decorating business has never rejected the classical altogether because its patrons have demanded traditional rooms. Is it because of this that the interior decorator is looked down on by the architect and those interested in art history? Or is it because women, on the initiative of Elsie de Wolfe, have come to enjoy an important role in the business? Is it for the same reason that it has escaped the attention of the art historian? We obtain a false impression of architecture if, in concentrating on the architect, we neglect the decorator. The great firms of the turn of the century, Allard, Alavoine, White Allom, Baumgarten and Herter contributed more than the architect to the interiors of houses, clubs and hotels. Nor should the role of the great emporiums be passed over, especially W. and J. Sloane of New York and Marshall Field of Chicago, when looking at interiors.

What crafts have been saved in our time from the dessicating blast of modern art has been due to the interior decorator and the client; they sustained and still sustain what is left of the crafts. Where would be the makers of wallpaper, wrought iron, upholstery, curtains, carved wood, plaster work, and the others who contribute to the interior? As for the crafts dependent on the architect, such as stone carving, they have virtually disappeared. Only through such training programs as those of *Restore* of the Municipal Art Society of New York, of the Cathedral of Saint John the Divine, New York, and of the Indiana Limestone Company of Bloomington is the craft being kept alive. (For example, a man desiring balusters for a balustrade for the roof of his house recently had them turned in Quebec.)

Not all architects joined in hounding the craftsmen from architecture. Along with the interior decorator a small band of architects has pursued the classical tradition, quietly and unostentatiously. In fact, their presence is peculiar to American architecture because they are found in no other Western country. A man like the late Mott B. Schmidt of New York, who died in 1977, remained loyal to the classical. So has Philip Trammell Shutze of Atlanta. Samuel Wilson, Jr., of Koch and Wilson of New Orleans, has completed a variety of classical buildings. G. Frederick Poehler of Sharon, Connecticut, has clients who demand the traditional. John Barrington Bayley has done possibly the finest classical building in recent years, the new wing of the Frick Collection in New York. Among the younger men, John Blatteau of Philadelphia, Norman Hubbert of San Francisco, and Allan Greenberg of New Haven design in the classical mode as has the firm of Easton and La Rocca of New York.

If we turn to the architectural and art schools, to the colleges and the universities, we discover that, until very recently, there was little sustaining of the classical. It is hard to grasp the ruthlessness with which modern art moved through the academic world. Consider the architectural schools. One of their distinctions two generations ago was their collections of casts of classical detail with some of the Gothic and Romanesque. (In art schools the casts of great Greek, Roman, and Renaissance statues were standard equipment.) Starting in the late 1930s, as the schools came to be headed by deans messianic in their modernism, the casts disappeared. It was a version of artistic "book-burning," and it also afflicted the art museums. Art history, a young field of learning even in the 1930s, began to present modern art as the path of progress, disregarding the obvious fact there is no such element as progress in art. The classical tradition was relegated to the world of the dead and accepted only as part of the history of ideas.

The first break in this interpretation in the world of the academe was an exhibition mounted in 1953 at the Yale University Art Gallery by the late Christopher Tunnard and Lamont Moore. Called *Ars in Urbe,* it explored the shaping of the city by the classical tradition, the object being to show that here was a major, if neglected, resource. (The reward for the organizers was to be savaged by the art critic of *The New York Times.* It was a case of being prematurely pro-classical.) What has occurred since has been very timid, and with reason, because the opposition was and is powerful. This refusal to accept the traditional is underscored by the fact that the only instruction in perspective and composition from the classical point of view and in the drafting of the orders and classical ornament is being offered by Classical America, the society founded in 1968 to encourage the classical tradition in the arts of this country.

True, the tradition has lately found some acceptance. But the acceptance must be treated with caution. The word "classical" is what has been made current rather than the tradition itself. Ever since the 1930s the custom has been for museum curators to re-baptize artistic movements of the past. Dealers will describe painters of our time as "Modern Old Masters." Buildings which would have been called variations on the modern a decade ago are now hailed as classical.

This brings us back to the matter of definition. It must be asserted again and again that what distinguishes the tradition is the presence of ornament, including human, animal (lion mask and dolphin) and vegetable (acanthus and laurel) forms and that this ornament is not Art Nouveau, nor Arabic, nor Egyptian, nor Gothic but classical. The master standard remains a building where all the arts have made a contribution, and the closest example we Americans have is our National Capitol.

If we come back to that great building, it is not only to point to it as a standard or a measure but also to remind ourselves that the classical of today will always be judged in terms of the past. (One of the attractions of modern art when new was that it excluded such comparisons.) In giving new life to this, the main current of Western art, in painting as well as architecture, in sculpture as well as furniture, in wrought iron along with bronze work, we have a long way to go.

Henry Hope Reed
President, Classical America

28. Beeby, *House of Poliphilos*, 1977, cat. 1.

ARCHITECTI • VITAE • VERBA

THOMAS H. BEEBY

Thomas H. Beeby, born in Oak Park, Illinois, in 1941 obtained his Bachelor of Architecture degree from Cornell University in 1964, having studied under Colin Rowe and John Hejduk. From Yale, where he subsequently studied with Paul Rudolph, Vincent Scully and Serge Chermayeff, he received his Master's of Architecture in 1965. He was an associate with C. F. Murphy Associates, Chicago, and is now a partner in Hammond Beeby and Babka in the same city. He has participated in exhibitions since 1976, notably in Munich, Chicago, New York, Minneapolis and Venice. He has been four times the recipient of the Distinguished Building Award of the American Institute of Architects, Chicago Chapter. In 1973 he joined the Department of Architecture of the Illinois Institute of Technology, Chicago. He is presently director of the School of Architecture, College of Architecture, Art and Urban Sciences, University of Illinois at Chicago Circle.

Classicism is the dominant style of Western architecture. It has permeated so deeply into our culture that even those in opposition to its authenticity are forced to speak its language in reaction rather than create a new vocabulary. The language of classicism evolved over many centuries and varies considerably from period to period; however, the formal relationship of parts has become the basis of our aesthetic sensibility. Simultaneously, the symbolic basis of architecture is embodied in the forms of classical architecture. At the most universal level it provides archetypal images related to the sacred art of building. Cultural values shared by society are transmitted through evocative forms of historical credibility. Finally, at a more personal level, local tradition and private reflection are possible through the inherent suppleness of the vocabulary. To erase classicism intentionally as suggested by modernism would seem to be an act of spiritual suicide as well as an impossibility.

JOHN BLATTEAU

John Blatteau, born in Philadelphia in 1943, received a degree in architecture from the University of Pennsylvania in 1971. He has taught at the same institution since 1976 and at Drexel University since 1978. At present he is with the firm Ewing Cole Cherry Parsky of Philadelphia. His design for Bayonne Hospital, Bayonne, New Jersey, received a Citation of Merit from Progressive Architecture *in 1980. His work has been recently exhibited at the first International Exhibition of Architecture of the Venice Biennale. He is a contributor of introductory notes for the Classical America Edition of Hector d'Espouy's* Fragments from Greek and Roman Architecture.

At the turn of the century, the question of whether or not there was an indigenous American architecture was posed to some of the most influential architects in the country. In the lively debate ("An Unaffected School of Modern Architecture in America—Will It Come?" *T Square Club Journal,* Philadelphia, 1899) that followed, John Carrère, of Carrère and Hastings, gave the answer that seemed most appropriate: "This is the sort of thing which it is usual to look back upon, and not forward to."

Carrère concluded that there did not, in fact, exist an indigenous American architecture. At this safe historical distance, we can, however, say with certainty that it did exist and continues to exist, and that it clearly finds its strength and unity in the use of the classical language of architecture and in its faithfulness to classical models. Ours is an architecture first of principle and, only secondly, of style.

An enormous part of the work of the office of Ewing Cole Cherry Parsky involves the design of institutional buildings. These projects are complex both in program and in the difficulties of the site. The classical language of architecture offers great potential in meeting the functional as well as the aesthetic demands inspired by these projects.

It is an architecture which addresses itself naturally to the issues of large-scale public buildings. The client and the public intuitively understand this language and respond positively to its beauty and its civic meaning. At the same time, this classical vocabulary offers the architect unlimited resources with which to meet the challenge of civic architecture. Texture, scale, dimension and detail can all be manipulated in the service of beauty.

Bayonne Hospital. In its design, Bayonne Hospital raises the critical issue of style within the framework of a complicated and technically demanding building program. The design ties together the physical plant of the existing hospital and reestablishes its physical identity in Bayonne. The classical style is used to reinforce this sense of identity.

By using elements traditionally common to public buildings, we reaffirm the civic aspect of the hospital in the community. Traditional elements of architecture are used in a traditional way, and a sense of human scale is restored to an institution which has tended in the past towards the cold and impersonal.

The resolution of the building at the base, with the use of rustication, dentils and keystones, enhances the pedestrian's experience of the building. Against the sky, the attic story cornice and rusticated mechanical penthouse complete the composition of the building.

Bayonne Hospital demonstrates that a traditional approach to design is a reasonable architectural alternative today. It also demonstrates that, given the option, clients respond warmly to an architecture based on tradition.

Holy Redeemer Hospital. Built in the early 1950s, Holy Redeemer Hospital has undergone several additions, the latest of which is a project consisting of the addition of a new twenty-four bed ICU/CCU and a new Emergency Department.

The program calls for the ICU/CCU to be located at the second floor level, in front of the original hospital building. This location, by displacing the main hospital entrance, gives special significance to the ICU/CCU addition. This building now becomes the symbolic entrance to the hospital and, by its location at the main highway, imparts to the hospital a new image.

The architectural solution calls for a rusticated ground floor of stone and a second floor of brick and stone. The rusticated ground floor will function in this phase of the project as a covered drive, while in the future this floor may well be reclaimed for administrative functions. The arched openings will then be glazed, and the main entrance moved to the front of the building.

PETER L. GLUCK

Peter L. Gluck, born in New York City in 1939, received his Bachelor of Arts degree from Yale University in 1962 and his Bachelor of Architecture degree from the same institution in 1965. Since 1972 he has been a principal with Peter L. Gluck and Associates, New York, New York. He has been an adjunct assistant professor at Columbia University as well as the director of Columbia's Japan Study Center. He received Industrial Design's *Award of Excellence in 1972 for his project for Bolton Valley prefabricated housing and in 1973 his House on a Lake was* Architectural Record's *House of the Year.*

House in Lincoln, Massachusetts. The form of this house is a response to a set of specific design and programmatic requirements generated by the family living there and the overall physical setting in which the house is situated.

Classical elements are part of that response and serve several purposes. The classically simple front façade with cornice, columns and pedimented gable is meant to recall things that are familiar to those who pass by or to those who come to visit. Lincoln, Massachusetts, is in that historically conscious area of New England where "traditional" design is revered, where "colonial" is the accepted style, and where the early American salt box still means house. While reassuringly simple from afar or at first glance, the composed elements reveal on closer inspection that they are by no means an attempt at strict historic re-creation, nor is there any desire to achieve historic accuracy. In fact, intentional anomalies in the composition do provide cues to the very personal and special private lives within.

The classical façade, in elevation looking almost like a child's drawing, becomes a reductive veil that simplifies the complicated object, infusing it with innocence.

MICHAEL GRAVES

Michael Graves was born in Indianapolis, Indiana, in 1934. In 1958 he received the Bachelor of Architecture degree from the University of Cincinnati, Ohio, and the Master of Architecture degree from Harvard University the following year. From 1960 to 1962, he was in residence at the American Academy in Rome as the recipient of the Prix de Rome *and the Brunner Fellowship. He is professor of architecture at Princeton University, where he*

NORTH VIEW

29. P. L. Gluck and Associates, *House,
Lincoln, Massachusetts,* 1977–80, cat. 14.

Facade from Hunter creek
south
Aspen house
Graves

30. Graves, *House in Aspen*, south façade, 1978, cat. 20.

has taught since 1963, and has been visiting professor at universities in New York, Los Angeles, Houston, and Austin. His work has been exhibited internationally and he is the six-time recipient of the Design Award from Progressive Architecture. *In 1975, he received the National Honor Award from the American Institute of Architects. Mr. Graves has been a principal in the firm, Michael Graves, Architect, Princeton, since 1964.*

When asked why I use classical elements in my work, I would prefer to speak of elements rather than classical elements, as I find that a somewhat loaded proposition. One might consider elements themselves as archetypal rather than as established only in classicism. I think it would be more appropriate to address the question to some modern architects and ask how it is in their work that the elements, which would have to be regarded as the language, our ability to speak, are not only disguised, but in some cases, nonexistent. There are certain phrases which have become common today, phrases such as "window wall," which, in language of architecture, would have to be regarded as visual slang.

If one sees the language of architecture as represented by those elements which are germane primarily—shall we say only—to architecture, then one has difficulty imagining an architectural composition without them. Those elements are simple things, but in combination with each other they establish both the pragmatic and symbolic language of an architectural culture. If I were to say that those elements that are so well known to us—such as wall, door, window, column, floor, ceiling—give us as architects an ability to express the culture physically and symbolically, most laymen would agree. However, somewhere in the recent past, the architectural question was dramatically altered. Instead of having a language built upon expressive elements relating to and having their roots in both man and nature, some would have us believe that it is better to wipe the slate clean.

Architecture has inverted the question somewhat in that many regard the idea of space or void as primary without much interest in or understanding of the enclosures and elements which give character or symbolic substance to space. A good example would be any of the many endless space-framed structures which, I believe, not only are disorienting but also limit our ability to make symbolic distinctions and hierarchies, or to give metaphorical substance to the room itself. If one were to contrast such a spaceless milieu with a typical eighteenth-century drawing room, which makes both pragmatic and symbolic distinctions between the elements and surfaces, one begins

to understand our current inability to speak a language when that language has been minimalized to the point of saying only one thing.

House in Aspen, Colorado. This large vacation house is to be used by one family with frequent guests. Because the house will not be occupied year-round, it is also necessary to provide quarters for full-time staff.

The site is located at the confluence of two small rivers and therefore the primacy of this intersection becomes exceedingly important in the location and orientation of the complex. The main house is oriented toward the south light and faces one of the two rivers, while the guest house is oriented east and faces the other river. These two arms provide the basis for the complex to be organized around a central court. The third side of the court is composed of staff quarters and storage buildings and the fourth side gives access to the pool and orchard.

The exterior wall surfaces of the building employ local wood log-cabin construction but reinterpret that vernacular within a more classical organization. The strong wooden base provides a visual link to the ground, while the remaining face of the building is seen as more ephemeral and frankly analogous to the surrounding landscape. The center section of the building is capped by a roof that not only gives importance to the central mass but also provides a sense of enclosure within the great hall below.

Red River Valley Heritage Interpretive Center. One of the most important aspects of the Red River Valley Heritage Interpretive Center is its particular urban setting in that the building is located in a pastoral garden at the edge of the Red River. Within the boundaries of both Fargo and Moorhead, it suggests the complementary themes inherent in urban and rural life, both of which are part of this institution.

The building itself is organized in a way which supports the thematic continuity and linearity of the story to be told. Upon entering, the visitor is given an option of beginning the exhibition sequence or attending an orientation presentation in the small lecture hall. The exhibition galleries are arranged in a loop that surrounds the center of the building which allows the visitor to relate his present location to the entire sequence, for there is exterior orientation and light available as he passes through the various exhibits. The relationship of the building to the outdoors is also crucial to this sequence, especially for an institution which helps describe and educate us relative to our beginnings on the land. The various outlooks

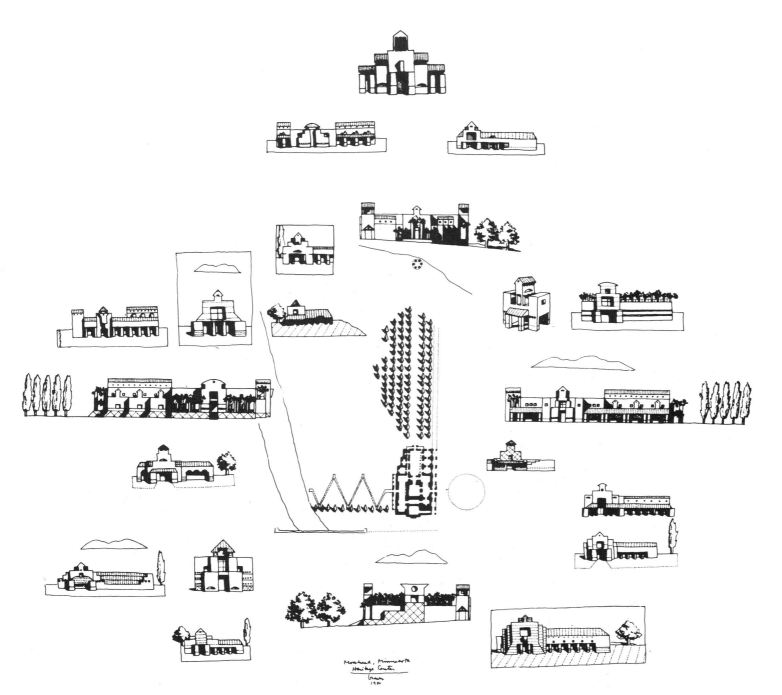

31. Graves, *Red River Valley Heritage Interpretive Center*, 1980, cat. 24.

from building to landscape help to reinforce the relationship of man to landscape.

Beyond the primary exhibition areas which offer a variety of spaces and light quality, temporary or changing exhibition space for traveling shows is located on the ground floor. Also, the administrative offices, library and oral history collection, and conference rooms are located around the central lecture hall core.

The building's character is known through our understanding of what we might regard as both an urban institution and rural vernacular. It is in this purposeful double reading that the culture of man and his roots, both urban and rural, are further enhanced.

ALLAN GREENBERG

Allan Greenberg was born in Johannesburg, South Africa, in 1938 and became a United States citizen in 1973. He received the Bachelor of Architecture degree from the University of the Witwatersrand, Johannesburg, in 1961 and the Master of Architecture degree from Yale University in 1965. He was a member of the faculty of the Yale Architecture School from 1969 to 1974 and was associate professor in the Department of Architecture at the University of Pennsylvania from 1975 to 1978. From 1967 to 1978, he was consultant to the Judicial Department of the State of Connecticut. Mr. Greenberg has been in private practice since 1967 and recently participated in the Venice Biennale in 1980.

The meaning of our architectural past is more complicated than simply duplicating or distorting the forms bequeathed to us by history. As a tradition, it is the vehicle through which we embody our systems of social, political, and religious norms. This is accomplished by means of typologies of buildings which are continuously modified as circumstances in society change. These building types provide a range of expressive and functional solutions to architectural problems.

It is the role of the architect to aid in the realization of society's aspirations by designing buildings which express the meaning and significance of the institutions they house. Architectural forms should facilitate, therefore, both the communication and the expression of these meanings. The most highly developed language of form available to us for this purpose is the classical language of architecture. Since antiquity, generations of architects have worked with the elements, grammar and meanings of classical architecture and adapted it to the needs of widely differing cultures, climates, and functions.

The use of precedent enabled both the architect and the client to incorporate the aesthetic and functional experience of the past into new solutions. For the great architects, this was liberating as it enabled them to master and expand the boundaries of the tradition; for the average practitioner, it provides a canon to design competent buildings, such as the great Georgian squares of London, Edinburgh and Boston. These buildings complement, rather than ignore or contrast with the extant architectural tradition.

The legacy of the past challenges us to create a fitting architecture for our times.

[Allan Greenberg, "The Meaning of the Past," *Sun and Moon, A Journal of Literature and Art* (Summer, 1980), p. 33.]

ROBERT L. HARPER

Robert L. Harper, born in 1939 in Rochester, New York, received the Bachelor of Arts degree from Amherst College in 1961 and the Master of Architecture degree from Columbia University in 1964. He was awarded the William Kinne Fellows Traveling Fellowship, which took him to Scotland in 1964–65. From 1965 to 1969, he was associated with Paul Mitarachi, Architects, New Haven, and subsequently with Charles W. Moore Associates, Essex, Connecticut, from 1969 to 1975. Since 1975, Mr. Harper has been the director of Moore Grover Harper, P.C., Architects and Planners, Essex.

Classical Forms in the Country House. Classical forms in architecture create certain expectations in the viewer. With Palladio's Villa Rotunda on its hilltop site, we see a familiar and stable relationship between villa and land though, through our prior experience, we can infer from the roof and porticoes what the villa's unseen sides and interior will be like. The Villa Barbaro is built against a hillside, but because the hill rises from front to back the house is seen in a stable relationship to its size and conforms, at least from this viewpoint, to our visual expectations.

The site of the country house is a long sloping meadow, easily accessible only from the south by moving along the side of the hill. The clients asked for major spaces, indoors and out, to be on one level. This determined a sequential arrangement of drive, car court,

32. Johnson, *The New Playhouse Theatre*, Cleveland, 1980–81, cat. 44.

house and pool court along the axis of movement across the site, with the meadow rising to the east and falling away to the west. The level floor of house and court along that axis is in strong and apparent contrast with the sloping plane of the site.

The use of classical forms in the country house makes possible the best visual exploitation of the contrast of house and land and the axial organization of the house itself. The classical forms produce expectations or preconceptions, but the site challenges them at once. As the building is experienced, some of these expectations are fulfilled and others are confounded, creating a visual richness that would not otherwise exist without classical references.

PHILIP JOHNSON

Philip Johnson was born in Cleveland, Ohio, in 1906. He received the Bachelor of Arts degree from Harvard University in 1930 and the Bachelor of Architecture degree from the Harvard Graduate School of Design in 1943. He was director of the Department of Architecture at the Museum of Modern Art, New York, from 1930 to 1936 and resumed the directorship from 1946 to 1954. He was a partner in the firm of Richard Foster, Philip Johnson and Richard Foster, New York, from 1964 to 1967 and has been a partner in Johnson/Burgee Architects, New York, since 1967. Mr. Johnson has been the recipient of numerous awards, including first prize at the Bienal Sao Paulo (1954) and the Twenty-Five Year Award (1975) and Gold Medal (1978) from the American Institute of Architects.

In my case, having been brought up by Mies van der Rohe—the Schinkel worshipper, then falling under the spell of Ledoux and Gilly—I was conditioned to classicism as a boy. And now that the International Style is no longer with us, a recourse to old habits seems only natural.

In the case of the Sugarland's office buildings, the program happened closely to fit the façade of the Feilner House, which I found in Schinkel's *Gesamte Werke*. I could not not copy. The relation of spandrel, stringcourse, window rhythm seemed aesthetically inevitable and functionally fitting. Compared to the thousands of boring glass cubes of Houston the design looks almost elegant and, incidentally, just as cheap.

The Cleveland Play House is quite different. The existing 1927 building is underscaled, vaguely Romanesquoid and very well de-signed indeed. When we were asked to join a larger unit with more lobbies, etc., a classical tempietto seemed the answer 1) to change scale at a mid-point 2) and to create a "familiar" entrance and focal point. In actuality, the size and most of the shape is Santa Costanza with a dash of Bernini at Ariccia and of Brunelleschi's Sacristy. The result is a pleasant confusion of periods which someday should give a sequential pleasure of procession around the various sides of the complex. A few octagonal crenellated towers add extra interest but are outside the theme of this exhibition.

ROBERT MICHAEL KLIMENT

Robert Michael Kliment, born in 1933 in Prague, Czecho-slovakia, received the Bachelor of Arts degree from Yale College in 1954 and the Master of Architecture degree from the Yale University School of Architecture in 1959. He spent 1959–60 as a Fulbright Scholar in Italy. From 1961 to 1971 he was in the office of Mitchell/Giurgola Associates, Architects, in New York; in 1972 he established R. M. Kliment Architect, New York, which in 1978 became R. M. Kliment & Frances Halsband Architects. Since 1976 he has been a consultant to the Technical Assistance Program of the New York State Council on the Arts, and since 1978 a member of the Architecture Advisory Committee of the Cooper-Hewitt Museum of the Smithsonian Institution in New York City. He has taught at the graduate schools of the University of Pennsylvania, Columbia University and M.I.T., and has been visiting critic at the University of Virginia and at Yale, Rice, North Carolina State and Harvard universities.

FRANCES HALSBAND

Frances Halsband, born in 1943 in New York City, received her undergraduate degree from Swarthmore College in 1965 and in 1968 a Master of Architecture from the Columbia University Graduate School of Architecture and Planning. In 1968 she joined the office of Mitchell/Giurgola Associates, Architects, in New York, in 1972 that of R. M. Kliment Architect, also in New York, and in 1978 became a partner in R. M. Kliment & Frances Halsband Architects. From 1975 to 1978 Ms. Halsband served on the Executive Board of the Architectural League of New York, from 1978 to 1980 on the Architecture

Advisory Committee of New York's Cooper-Hewitt Museum of the Smithsonian Institution, and from 1979 to 1980 she was the Secretary of the Executive Committee of the American Institute of Architects, New York chapter. Since 1975 she has been a consultant to the Technical Assistance Program of the New York Council on the Arts, and since 1978 has been the secretary of the Architectural League of New York's Executive Board. She has been a lecturer in architectural design at Columbia University and Barnard College and a visiting critic at the University of Virginia and Rice and Harvard universities.

Clarity of organization and serenity of spirit are the classically-inspired goals of our projects. Plans are organized hierarchically to establish orientation. Hierarchy is developed by varying intensity and complexity of elaboration of detail and ornament.

A classically derived order of visual elements forms a cultural and architectural connection from past to present. Our work embodies humanist perceptions of the cultural context.

Connection with and continuing development of a cultural and architectural tradition, rather than style or decoration for its own sake, forms the basis of our work.

EDWARD S. LEVIN

Edward S. Levin was born in 1952, in Schenectady, New York. In 1974, he received the Bachelor of Architecture degree from Cornell University, where he was awarded the Otto R. Eggers Memorial Prize by the Department of Architecture; in 1975 he was granted the Master in Architecture degree from Harvard University. He taught architecture at Carnegie-Mellon University from 1975 to 1979. At present, he is assistant professor of architecture at Syracuse University. His professional affiliations include Day & Zimmer Associates, Philadelphia (1973), Herman & Lees Associates, Cambridge, Massachusetts (1975), and L. P. Perfido Associates, Pittsburgh (1978).

A fundamental issue which concerns me, and which my work seeks to address, is the condition of architecture after modernism. If it has now become obvious that part of the legacy of modern architecture is an impoverishment of architectural language, and if it seems obvious as well that one of the remedies for this condition must involve the connection of architecture to its pre-modern past, it must be equally clear that any attempt at the recuperation of historical form will be seen *within the context of modernism itself*. Such a recognition must surely preclude any *unself-conscious* applications of pre-modern form, and must consequently lead either to the abstraction and reduction of historical elements, or to the manipulation and deformation of the elements within their various systems.

It is this latter attitude—in effect an investigation into *language*—which underlies allusions to classical vocabulary in both of the projects shown here: *An American Standard Home* and *A Solar Greek-Revival House*. Although classical language is not the only pre-modern one which I employ in my work, it is, I am convinced, that architectural vocabulary which is most susceptible to manipulation, primarily because of the precise codification it has received through history, and therefore its recognition as *always having been* a codified language.

I am also concerned with that long-standing and peculiarly *American* phenomenon of the importation of European architecture as "proof of our national good taste" (according to Thomas Jefferson), despite the inevitable alteration of that architecture after its arrival here. American architects have consistently been capable (and still remain so) of *re-presenting* even the most "foreign" of precedents in the pragmatic garb of native American technology; the unintended side effects of these alterations is an important part of the subject of both *An American Standard Home* and *A Solar Greek-Revival House*. Partly as a critique of this American penchant for "adaptation," and partly because available technology makes the "correct" brand of classicism untenable—if not impossible altogether—both of my projects address classicism in a deliberately ironic manner. Indeed, it seems to me that irony is indispensable to any attempt to use classical vocabulary today, for even if irony is not at the *core* of such intentions, it will assuredly surface in any attempt to reassert an "authentic" classicism. The lesson in this is, of course, that if the object is not clearly *intended* as ironic, it can only become the *object* of irony itself.

RODOLFO MACHADO

Rodolfo Machado, born in Argentina in 1942, is a citizen of the United States. He received the Diploma in Architecture from the Universidad de Buenos Aires in 1966, and studied urban design at the Centre de Recherche d'Urbanisme in Paris from 1967 to 1968. In 1970 he received the Master of Architecture degree from the University of California at Berkeley, where he continued with doctoral studies in architectural theory until 1973. Mr.

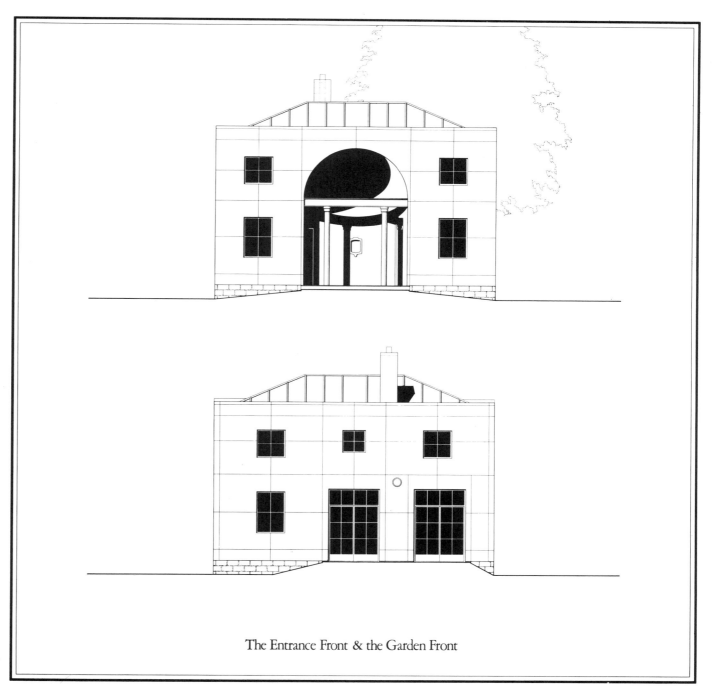

The Entrance Front & the Garden Front

33. Levin, *An American Standard Home,* 1979, cat. 60.

34. Machado and Silvetti, *The Steps of Providence,* 1979, cat. 67.

Machado has taught at the University of California at Berkeley and Carnegie-Mellon University and is currently head of the Department of Architecture at the Rhode Island School of Design. He has practiced architecture in San Francisco and Pittsburgh and is a principal in Machado-Silvetti, Boston. With Mr. Silvetti, he participated in the 1980 Venice Biennale.

JORGE SILVETTI

Jorge Silvetti, born in Buenos Aires, Argentina, in 1942, is a citizen of the United States. He received the Diploma in Architecture from the Facultad de Arquitectura, Universidad de Buenos Aires, in 1966; in 1969 he was granted the Master of Architecture degree from the University of California at Berkeley, where he pursued doctoral studies in architectural theory. He has held the position of associate professor of architecture at Harvard University since 1976 and has also taught at the University of California at Berkeley and Carnegie-Mellon University. He is presently a principal in Machado-Silvetti, Boston.

In our design for the Steps of Providence, no one single classical element in a "pure" state can be found. They are all transformations of classical motives, transformed to the point of being either aclassical or anticlassical. A distinction should be made between "classical elements" and "classical notions." The latter we use all the time; they are simply *architectural* notions," organizing principles, valid beyond the sometimes superficial distinctions between classicism and modernity.

Some recent stylistic manifestations using classical elements seem to confuse fundamental issues about what the *production* of architecture is or should be. Figurative choices, in which historical elements are evident, serve as a critique of modern architecture through the act of inversion. This is a typically avant-garde operation which will soon fall prey to our society's peculiar but overwhelming tendency to consume symbols as quickly as they are created.

We prefer a method that demonstrates the conceptual continuity and permanency of architecture. Instead of an easy, banal avant-garde inclusion of detail we would like to see a critique of the present state of architecture based on more solid and general notions about the production of form and meaning. The act of production unavoidably transforms that which is known; only through so doing can mutations occur and eventually genuine innovation result.

Our stand, therefore, is not stylistic. The presence of the architectural past is inevitable as well as unequivocal, and we have incorporated whatever part of it is valuable into our own "historical resources." We ignore the controversy between modernism and historicism to concentrate on the production of an architecture that effects its own clarification by resorting to principles that are beyond style.

HENRY L. MELTZER

Henry Meltzer was born in New York City in 1941 and received an undergraduate degree in art history from Columbia University and a graduate degree in architecture from the University of Pennsylvania. He worked for architectural firms in Philadelphia and New York prior to establishing practice as The Henry Meltzer Group, a health facilities consulting and architectural firm founded in 1974.

NICK BALLARD

Nick Ballard was born in New York City in 1942. He received both a Bachelor of Science in Electrical Engineering and a Master of Science in Management from the Polytechnic Institute of Brooklyn. A principal and general manager at The Henry Meltzer Group, he is responsible for the implementation and coordination for all projects.

LOUIS VIGORITO

Louis Vigorito, born in the province of Salerno, Italy, in 1959, moved to the United States in 1971. He attended the Cooper Union School of Architecture from 1977 to 1980. He is currently on a leave of absence from Cooper Union and working for The Henry Meltzer Group.

Our problem was to give character to an office in an early 1900s New York office building which has interesting classical exterior details and little interior detail of any kind.

We used classical elements in the design of our office because of the sense of scale, detail and associations they bring to a previously loftlike work environment. The entrance in particular is a readily identifiable symbol of our classical interests and of the importance of scale, tradition, elegance, substance, and humor in our work.

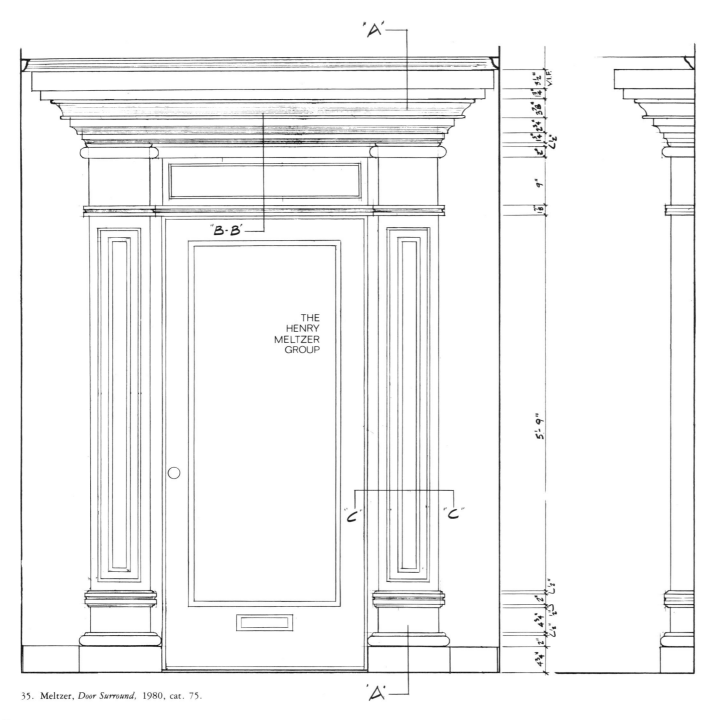

"A"

V.I.F.

THE
HENRY
MELTZER
GROUP

"B·B"

"C"   "C"

"A"

35. Meltzer, *Door Surround,* 1980, cat. 75.

CHARLES W. MOORE

Born in Benton Harbor, Michigan, in 1925, Charles W. Moore received the Bachelor of Architecture degree from the University of Michigan in 1947 and the Master of Fine Arts and Ph.D. from Princeton University. He has taught at the University of Utah in Salt Lake City, at Princeton University and was chairman of the Departments of Architecture at the University of California at Berkeley (1962–65) and at Yale University (1965–69), where he was also Dean of the School of Architecture (1969–71). Since 1975 he has been professor of architecture at UCLA and was appointed program head in the School of Architecture in 1978. From 1970 to 1975 he was a principal in Charles W. Moore Associates and has been a partner in Moore Grover Harper, Essex, Connecticut, since 1975 and a partner in Moore, Ruble, Yudell, Los Angeles, since 1977. He has also worked with Urban Innovations Group since 1975. In 1980, he participated in the Venice Biennale.

Even when we try to avoid having a language of architecture, we wind up with one. We all, in our separate ways, use style, and we design our buildings, perhaps with style, certainly in one or more styles. If we are altogether dissatisfied with what we see around us, we may try to devise an entirely new style, a kind of architectural Esperanto, but untried new languages generally have flaws. (Some flaws of the modern architectural idiom have been much discussed: you can't find the front door, and the roof leaks.) So Esperanto dies out, and the incomparably rich heritage of 2,500 years of Latin and post-Latin languages, redolent of all the amazing things they have conveyed to us reasserts itself. We have as well an architectural heritage of posts and beams and roofs and walls, all carefully developed over time to stand and withstand the elements. It is still there to transmit complete signals to us.

The recent past is instructively full of examples of how delicate those signals can be and still transmit. My favorite single line in a building is a thin incision Karl Friedrich Schinkel made in the flat surfaces most of the way up the wall, in his pavilion at Charlottenberg. It hints at the ancient distinctions between shaft and entablature, and energizes, with the energy of a well-loved past, the whole building.

Our buildings try, with less of the rapier and more of the bulldozer, to emulate this stroke.

Sammis Hall. A part of the Banbury Conference Center complex, Sammis Hall is a sixteen-bedroom building for scientists attending several day or week-long research seminars. The bedrooms, also used as study and private retreat, surround a skylighted, two-story miniature "Great Hall" or rotunda which will be used for small discussion groups as well as an informal living room. The hall is enlivened by sets of abstract arches which frame the main stair and float below the skylights. Pairs of bedrooms are entered from a buffer hallway and share a bath.

The site is a large, landscaped Long Island estate. The main approach to Sammis Hall will be axial on a walking path between two rows of gnarled, old apple trees. The design responds to this implied formality through the use of symmetry and the inspiration of Palladio to achieve a suitably dignified image.

CHRISTOPHER MORRIS, TIMOTHY MORRIS

Christopher and Timothy Morris (identical twins), born in 1952, obtained Bachelor of Science degrees in Architecture at the University of Virginia in 1975. Christopher received his Master's of Architecture from Princeton in 1978 while Timothy received his Master's of Architecture from Yale in 1978. As students they have won awards both as a team and individually and their work since graduation has been exhibited at Harvard and the University of Kentucky. A show is planned for Rensselaer Polytechnical Institute next fall. As a design team Morris & Morris is primarily concerned with the marriage of solar technology and architectural aesthetics, and the exploration of "high-style" furniture for the minimalist apartment. Both are employed at Drummey, Rosane & Anderson Inc. in Newton Center, Massachusetts, Timothy since 1979 and Christopher as a consultant since 1980. In addition they practice independently in Westchester and Fairfield counties in the New York-Connecticut area.

Classical Vocabularies in the Passive Solar Home: Their Inclusion and Intention. Solar technologies and architectural aesthetics have for too long been unsuccessfully combined. Application of the historical precedents of form, ruling symmetry, and traditional ornament to a basic solar collective, trombe-wall concept unites classical theme and energy efficiency.

The pedimented south façade and the classical arrangement of the four columns at its base become technical as well as ornamental contributions. The canvas *velarium* also contains determinants which are twofold. While the style explicitly evokes associations and romantic allusions to the past, the form and function of these elements and the spaces they reinforce become necessary technical devices which manipulate convection loop strategies vital in the passive solar envelope system.

Expansion and Flexibility Criteria. As the architects, it is our intention to incorporate a complete solar energized system into a simple, formalized, and vernacular structure. Solar efficiencies and the architectural aesthetic have for too long been unsuccessfully combined. Previous attempts and failures have restricted the home builder to choose either one or the other. The combination has been thought to be uncompromisingly impossible. How can a solar home be designed with an associable vernacular integrity? Our house marries the formalistic and classical theme of a house to a successful solar energized function. This union is aesthetically achieved by formalizing the basic solar concept with components of symmetry, ornament and the vernacular form.

A simple structure and compactness of centralized plan with minimal perimeter maximizes efficiency and economy. Through innovative design using basic materials (as specified in the *solarium* shell) expensive and custom-shop work required for most greenhouse structures can be avoided. While designed to make maximum use of the sun, other architectural vocabularies of sloped roof, central entry, chimney, classical detailing all yield a design identifiable and attractive to the home buyer.

Our house is marketable for both high and low density housing. Blank east and west elevations allow for row-house arrangement for urbanistic properties, as well as sensible and coordinated additions in a rural setting. A simple twelve foot by twenty foot addition can turn a flexible two to three bedroom basic design unit into as much as a five-bedroom house, in which a new bathroom may serve the den-bedroom option as well as the new bedroom. An addition of a carport on one side of the house aesthetically complements the bedroom expansion on the other side and adds harmony to the overall plan. For economical reasons the two upstairs bathrooms share a huge bathtub beneath the central skylight and alongside the glass-block slit in the wall. (for greater privacy, ample space is allowed for two separate tubs). As a successful prototype, the house still offers flexibility in design.

Richness and artistic values are obtained through application of ornament and color on the simple shell. Choice of detailing may help to personalize façades on similar structural frames. Articulation of functional detailing of gutters, skylights, shutters, lights and other aesthetical additives of color, lattice-work pilasters and trim offers each house its own creative identity. The façadal treatment of individual houses depends upon the home owner's choice of functional and aesthetic ornament. The exciting and innovative function of the *velarium* on the south façade or the lattice work on the north are just two of the house's decorative possibilities.

Minimal mechanical costs enhance economical characteristics of simplification of structure and plan. A growing family will value the flexibility of the basic unit and its allowance for expansion. Our house is the prototype which may relieve the heavy monetary demands made on today's home buyer. Our house ends the search for the better way to live.

The Energy Conservation Criteria. The house in general takes a traditionally American compact configuration to reduce heat loss. The arrangement of the plan is such that the main living spaces are located on the south side whereas the compact functional rooms are located on the north wall. The location of the stair in the spatially separate *solarium* as opposed to the main volume of the house helps solve the common heat stratification problems associated with two-story houses.

Trees are planted, with the prevailing winter winds taken into account, to act as wind breaks. Earth berming on the north, east, and west façades enhances insulation, and can be seen as an accommodation to a sloping site.

Heat from the sun is collected passively via a sunspace and a trombe wall in front of each bedroom. Thermal storage in the sunspace is provided by the darkly painted twelve-inch concrete block wall filled with grout and by the eight-inch poured concrete floor. Additional storage, which can be considered optional, is provided by four columns of triple-stacked black steel water drums.

Excess heat from the sunspace pyramids up with the aid of a blower through the central area of the roof and down the north wall air plenum to a gravel bed storage below the house where the air releases its heat before returning to the sunspace. Excess heat can also be funneled up the peak from the trombe wall if necessary. To prevent potential overheating from the roof aperture on the north side of the bedrooms, operable vents open up to the air plenum so that this excess heat can be stored in the gravel bed.

During the night, cooled air from the sunspace drops while the warm air from the gravel bed rises up the north wall and through vents to the bedrooms. Additional heat radiates from the warm floor just above the gravel bed.

Heat loss through the exterior four-inch or six-inch stud walls is

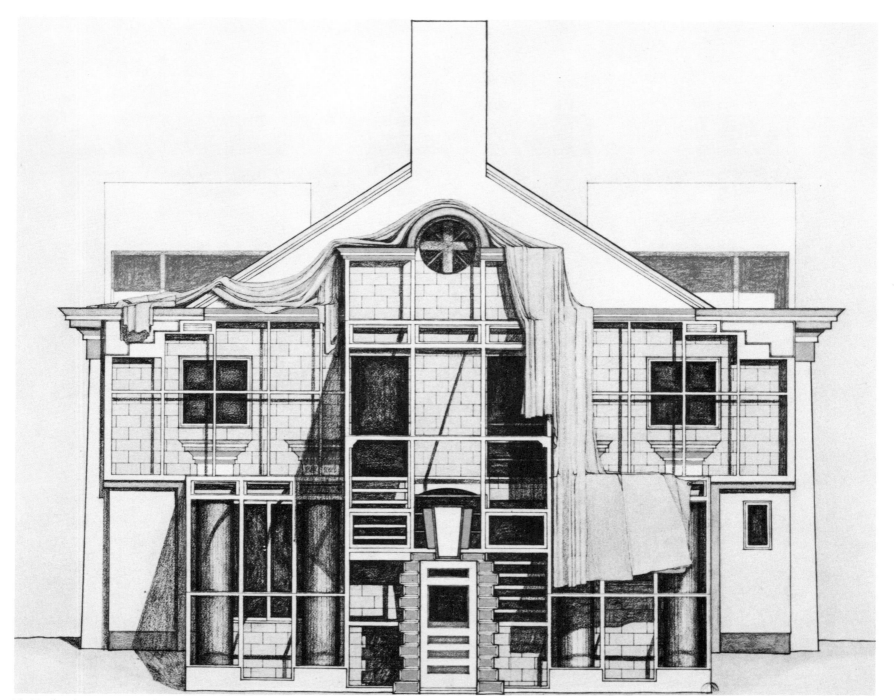

36. Morris and Morris, *Passive Solar Home*, 1979, cat. 85.

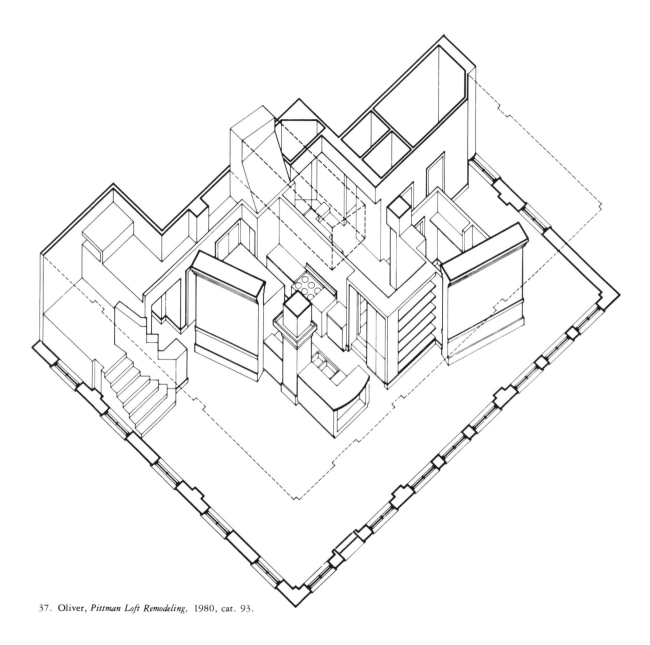

37. Oliver, *Pittman Loft Remodeling*, 1980, cat. 93.

reduced by insulation which would vary for different regions of the country. Operable insulating shutters or curtains would be recommended for all windows at night as well as in the daytime on the north side. The sunspace can be completely closed off from the house at night.

A conventional back-up heating system (preferably an oil/wood burning furnace) would distribute heat through a single duct hanging from the first floor ceiling. Back-up heat can also be provided by the study fireplace.

During the summer season operable windows and doors strategically placed high and low in the walls and *solarium* maximize cross-ventilation cooling as well as night cooling of thermal mass. The cooling system is assisted in extreme conditions by an exhaust fan located at the top of the mass wall.

The use of insulating shutters or curtains as well as the planting of deciduous trees provide shade during the summer days. A *velarium* gives shade when drawn over the *solarium*.

RICHARD B. OLIVER

Richard B. Oliver was born in 1942 in San Diego, California. He received the Bachelor of Architecture degree from the College of Environmental Design, University of California at Berkeley, in 1965, and was awarded a Fulbright Scholarship to Cambridge University, England, for 1965–66. In 1967, he was granted the Master of Architecture degree from the University of Pennsylvania, where he was the recipient of the Haney Fellowship in Architecture for 1966–67. He has held academic positions at the University of Texas at Austin, where he was assistant professor in the School of Architecture from 1967 to 1970, and at the School of Architecture and Urban Planning at UCLA, and has served as visiting studio critic for these and other universities. Mr. Oliver has been associated with Richard Meier & Associates, New York, and was a partner in the firm of Meltzer-Oliver-Solomon, New York, from 1976 to 1979. From 1977 to 1980 he was curator of architecture and design at the Cooper-Hewitt Museum, New York. Since 1980, he has maintained a private practice in New York City.

Classical elements can enrich the conventional modern language of architecture. They can be used to manipulate and enhance the scale, spatial order, and sculptural effect of buildings and their interiors. I am interested in these more purely architectural effects of classicism

rather than in the aura of historical pedigree which classical elements also may impart. I prefer to design new elements which emulate the form and the feel of classical precedents rather than to reproduce elements found in patternbooks. In part, this reflects my preference for stripped, streamlined effects, and in part the difficulties of finding craftsmen to execute more elaborate work.

In the Pittman Loft, two large, free-standing pink walls are adorned with base molding, chair rail, and crown molding. One end of each wall is wrapped with these three elements and the other end of each wall is sliced away to reveal the sculptural qualities of the cross section of each molding. A third element is rendered as a free-standing column with an over-scaled capital, large enough to contain recessed uplights. These three architectural elements are painted in vivid colors to emphasize their primary position in the loft. Simple plain walls form a contrasting background to the three elements adorned with classical moldings.

STEVEN K. PETERSON

Steven K. Peterson was born in Indianapolis, Indiana, in 1940. In 1965 he received the Bachelor of Architecture degree from Cornell University, where he also studied Urban Design in 1969–70. Mr. Peterson is presently assistant professor of architecture at Columbia University, a position he has held since 1977, and maintains a private practice in New York City.

BARBARA LITTENBERG

Barbara Littenberg was born in New York City in 1949. She received the Bachelor of Architecture degree from Cornell University in 1971. From 1979 to 1981, she was design critic in architecture at the Columbia University School of Architecture and in 1981 Ms. Littenberg was named design critic in architecture at the Harvard University Graduate School of Design. She presently maintains a private practice in New York.

In the process of reincorporating classical allusion into architecture we must be careful not to reinstate the literal goals and compositional principles of classicism itself. It would be a mistake to assume that the rules and standards of classicism represent all or necessarily the best historical precedents. Further, classical planning rules are inadequate in the context of the current urban challenge, that of reconstructing the city's textures and spaces. Their use would only produce a false monumentality, an object fixation which is one of the most severely criticized aspects of the modern city.

Interweaving existing and new urban spaces requires a synthetic construction which will necessarily contain aspects of accident and disorder. A compound urban fabric always has the capacity to satisfy itself functionally, with alternative interpretations being sponsored by mere proximity of form and variety of place. Some tactics we have chosen to achieve this multi-use texture include the use of discontinuous figural space as opposed to continuous void, the design of dwellings as part of complex blocks rather than as objectified housing units, and the establishment of alternative design fields deliberately smaller or larger than the available site. This will produce a series of overlapping solutions appropriate to themselves yet responsive to the continuities beyond. This density of texture provides linkages and separations of space more flexible than the nakedness of one single, open area.

The specific problem at Les Halles was not only a general reconstruction of the city fabric but the introduction of a major public space of metropolitan scale, two potentially contradictory objectives on a site this size. Accomplishing both seemed the unique challenge, one which precluded any narrow definition of classical composition. Rather, our strategy was to develop the whole area of the site as a composite precinct able to perform in complicated and deliberately ambiguous ways. The interior is a figural armature of volumetric space, the exterior is manifested in different ways according to various peripheral conditions. For example, the exhibition building which is part of the precinct presents itself to the south as a main façade rather like the walls of an ancient city. To the north and west, its walls become housing and its configuration is shaped to correspond with the form of adjacent streets and square.

The entire precinct is a symbol for the idea of city, conceived like a traditional walled city but in reverse. Historically, the city was contained within its walls, with the landscape outside. Here the walls contain the space of a protected garden while the city itself appears to expand beyond. This connotation of an archaeological city carved out of the interior of existing blocks is amplified by restricting access to the garden to four gates located at the cardinal points, so that the garden is structured like an original Roman town, but is at once garden and urban space.

The space of this composite precinct with its garden is in effect a hidden and perhaps mysterious place, meant to relate to all of the city. Its meaning is not specific, but is intended to represent, together with the exhibition building incorporated into it, the history of the city as a general idea.

JAMES STEWART POLSHEK

James Stewart Polshek was born in Akron, Ohio, in 1930. He received the Bachelor of Science degree from Case Western Reserve University, Cleveland, in 1951 and the Master of Architecture degree from Yale University School of Architecture, New Haven, in 1955. He was a Fulbright Fellow at the Royal Academy of Fine Arts, Copenhagen, in 1956–57. His professional affiliations have included I. M. Pei and Associates, New York (1955–56), and Ulrich Franzen and Associates, New York (1957–60). Since 1962, he has maintained a practice in New York as James Stewart Polshek and Associates. Mr. Polshek was vice president of the New York chapter of the American Institute of Architects in 1970–71 and has served as vice president of the Municipal Art Society in New York since 1974. He was named dean of the faculty of the Graduate School of Architecture and Planning, Columbia University, and special adviser to the President of Columbia for Planning and Development, in 1973 and presently continues in that appointment.

I have been particularly outspoken concerning what I believe of literal classical elements in design—the classicizing of architecture and the consequent diminishing of its importance to society. In Roget's *Thesaurus* "classical" has many meanings and they are useful to review.

classical: antiquarian, superannuated, antique, archaic
classical: perfected, finished, consummate
classical: model, exemplary, ideal
classical: elegant, tasteful, graceful, polished, refined, restrained, clear, simple, unaffected, natural, pure. . . .

It is the latter three of these definitions that I prefer to apply to my use of those architecturally expressive elements that are meant to increase one's delight and understanding of a given work. The oft-invoked rationale that historical allusions impute greater "meaning" to a given architectural work is frequently nonsense or wishful thinking. Historical connections that are meaningful to one person are meaningless to the next. Simplistic borrowing of classical motifs with the intention to "enrich" and therefore make more "popular" is too often used to obscure ignorance of the various basic architectural principles to which I will presently refer or, in more skilled hands

38. J. S. Polshek and Partners/P. L. Gluck and Associates, a joint venture, *Delafield Estate,* 1980, cat. 104.

(many of which are represented in this exhibition), to excuse the inadequacies of extant technology and our depleted economy. A further irony is that an architectural language whose very existence is dependent on referred visual judgment and technical virtuosity is being revived in an age in which the public's taste and regard for craftsmanship has virtually disappeared and in which an artisan class no longer exists.

That there is a "public" appetite for artifacts of the past is undisputed. But this more frequently takes the form of a sentimentalizing nostalgia than an authentic longing for true classical traditions. "Gay nineties" night clubs and ersatz "theme" parks such as Busch Gardens or Disneyland are a few of the more bizarre examples of this longing for another time.

What I believe does have meaning to people in an architectural work are those qualities that most often survive the changing tastes of various ages, those aspects of a building that have timeless values. It is useful here to refer to Rudolph Arnheim's *The Dynamics of Architectural Form* where in the introduction he says that "studies of popular taste are of interest to the social scientist and useful to the businessman. But to be meaningful, they must identify the particular properties inherent in the object [building] on which preference or rejection is based."

The qualities I referred to in the previous paragraph and the aspects and properties that Arnheim refers to include planar and volumetric proportion, scale, surface characteristics, circulation logic, visual cueing, relationships between horizontal and vertical and between solid and void. These constitute, for me, the true classical language of architecture. Vitruvius's "Firmness, Commodity and Delight" is more simply descriptive. In short, these elements of architecture taken separately and as an ensemble must create in the user or the passerby a sense of dignity, pride, congeniality and security, which, in the end, I believe to be the appropriate social role for buildings designed by architects.

THOMAS GORDON SMITH

Thomas Gordon Smith was born in Oakland, California, in 1948. He was granted the Bachelor of Art degree from the University of California at Berkeley in 1970 and the Master of Architecture degree from the same institution in 1975. He has taught architectural history at the College of Marin in Kentfield, California. In 1979, he received the Rome Prize in Architecture from the American Academy in Rome and participated in the Venice Biennale the following year. His work has been included in exhibitions at the Cooper-Hewitt Museum, the Art Institute of Chicago and museums in California. Mr. Smith is presently in private practice.

I use the classical elements of architecture for their formal beauty, sculptural malleability, and for their rich tradition of iconographic associations. One of my intentions is to employ these elements to represent ideas. During the past years, I have become increasingly aware of the importance of subject in my buildings and I have begun to use the elements of classical architecture to develop the subject, either metaphorically or iconographically, depending on the level of articulation which seems appropriate. For example, in two adjacent houses in Livermore, California, I used classical elements without specific iconographic associations to suggest a general idea, the Roman house. On the other hand, in the façade dedicated to *Architettura* for my exhibition at the 1980 Venice *Biennale,* I made an explicit statement of my views about architecture. I combined classical elements of high and low orders and incorporated an allegorical painting which distinguished between my architectural projects inspired by *Disegno* and those under the influence of *Errore.*

Currently, I am working to determine which aspects of the tradition of classical associations remain representational today, and which associations must be altered to have current validity. My intent is not to design buildings which are commentaries on the tradition of classical architecture, but rather to contribute to that vast and contradictory tradition.

Tuscan House and Laurentian House. Tuscan House and Laurentian House are a pair of adjacent houses which were built in 1979 in Livermore, California. The houses are named after two of Pliny's villas described in his letters. The houses are not intended to be reconstructions of the villas; they are meant to reflect the ambience of Pliny's descriptions. They are contemporary houses which reflect the values of a Roman house, many of which seem appropriate in California. I did not confine the imagery to first century Italy; however, the subject is developed by a number of ancient references. The plans and the asymmetrical distribution of the interior volumes and exterior masses are like the late antique houses in Ostia which, despite their confined sites, were built to suggest the grand vistas of Hadrian's Villa. A monumental element, such as the triumphal arch motif at the entrance to Laurentian House, emphasizes the ancient theme, but it is scaled down for domestic application. Although two cartouches contain imagery which relates to California, neither these

39. T. G. Smith, *Tuscan House and Laurentian House,* 1979–80, cat. 115.

nor the architectural members are articulated with a strong iconographic intent. Rather, they are developed to provide a sense of place.

The houses are strongly related to one another and are treated as a unit. The garage of the Laurentian House is detached to create three volumes which are complementary in form, style, and spatial relationships. The buildings cover much of the area of their small lots, but they are sited to achieve a maximum sense of openness. The major rooms in both houses open onto private courtyards from which vistas extend the sense of space. The "piazzetta" between the Laurentian House and its garage is oriented toward the arched courtyard of the Tuscan House. This strongly integrates the houses and allows the sun to penetrate to light the Tuscan courtyard and the living room beyond. Also, the exteriors of both houses are strong and evocative. The walls are in pastel tints (blue, rose, and yellow), the sculptural and architectural decoration in saturated color.

Although the rooms are distinct and defined, they are linked by corridors which allow a successive revelation of the interior. This is especially true in Tuscan House where the major rooms remain spatially defined despite the fact that they are all linked by the foyer and hall. The rooms are also differentiated by variations in the intensity of light, formality of planning, height and configuration of ceilings, and decorative treatment.

In Tuscan House and Laurentian House I have used classical elements metaphorically to suggest a general idea. In other projects I have relied on the tradition of meanings associated with classical elements to articulate more specific ideas.

ROBERT A. M. STERN

Robert A. M. Stern was born in New York City in 1939. He received the Bachelor of Arts degree from Columbia University in 1960 and the Master of Architecture degree from Yale University in 1965. He holds the position of associate professor at Columbia University, where he has taught since 1970, and was the William Henry Bishop Visiting Professor at Yale University in 1978. Mr. Stern has been program director of the Architectural League of New York (1965–66), president of the League (1973–77) and director of the New York chapter of the American Institute of Architects (1976–78). He has served in a variety of capacities as consultant and urban designer to the City of New York. In 1969 he became a partner in Robert A. M. Stern and John S. Hagmann, Architects, New York, and has been a principal in the firm, Robert A. M. Stern Architect, New York, since 1977. Mr. Stern has exhibited at the Cooper-Hewitt Museum, the Museum of Modern Art, and the Whitney Museum and participated in the Biennale *in 1980.*

Pluralism is the characteristic state of the modern (i.e., post-Renaissance) world, and in architecture the diversity and continuity of our traditions is represented in three expressive modes or paradigms which at once represent ideal and real conditions: the classical, the vernacular, and the mechanical. In order to represent the complex interaction of issues in modern life, post-Renaissance architecture has traditionally sought a synthesis of these modes.

Classicism in particular has two uses: syntactically, as an aid to composition, and rhetorically, as an aid to expression. Modernist architecture has rejected the representative use of classicism, concentrating instead on mechano-morphology. A genuine revitalisation of the classical tradition, however, one which sees it in the light of contemporary production techniques as well as inherited meanings, is capable of fostering an interaction between a clearly public architecture and the viewer's personal reservoir of images and associations, thereby encouraging a meaningful dialogue between the present and the past.

DOM Headquarters, Brühl, Germany. The DOM building is intended as a jewel and a strong box at once, a structure of diamondlike objectivity set apart from the rough industrial landscape, a working monument that incorporates in steel and reflective glass those qualities of precision that one associates with the products of the DOM corporation.

The plan consists of an office tower sitting upon a base housing the entrance hall, cafeteria and training facilities. The base relates in height to the low mass of the adjacent factory and its shape, that of two superimposed squares (set at a diagonal to one another), enhances the frontality of the tower on the entrance side while permitting it to be read more sculpturally in the round from the motor highway. The tower and the base are sheathed in tinted glass; the colors, green, black and silver are selected to enhance further the desired image of cool mechanical perfection.

While the design seeks to be forward-looking through its precise use of advanced construction technology, it also draws upon a rich tradition of modern classicism to place the building within a broad cultural and architectural context. Thus, the design seeks to continue and expand upon the technically advanced and classically composed building tradition established by Otto Wagner, Gropius and Meyer.

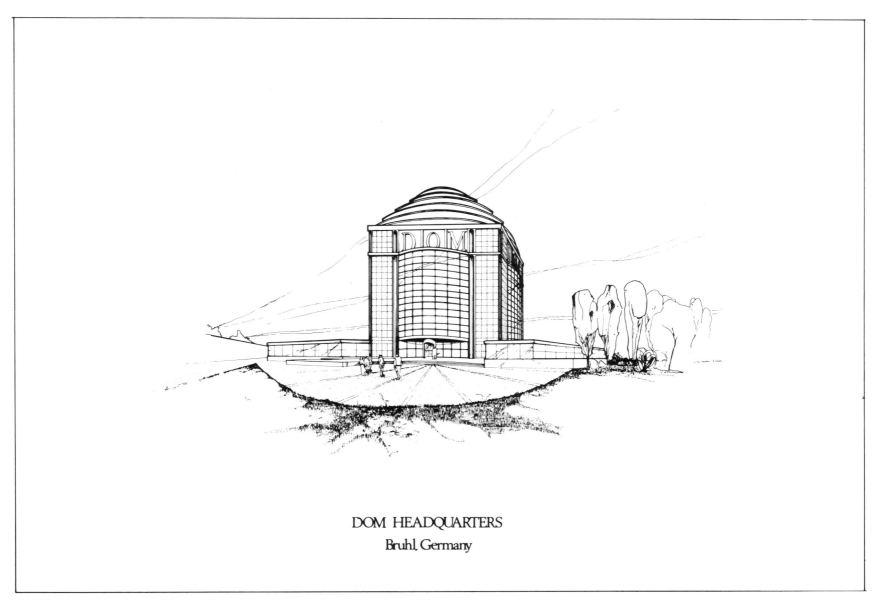

DOM HEADQUARTERS
Bruhl, Germany

40. Stern, *DOM Headquarters*, Brühl, Germany, 1980, cat. 119.

In its interior spaces the headquarters draws upon lessons from the commercial buildings of Frank Lloyd Wright. His Johnson Wax Headquarters is specifically referred to in the great reception hall/product presentation room at the top, a room that can become a major public space.

The tower is designed to be impressive by day and by night. Its principal feature is the stepped dome at its top which by day admits natural light to the product presentation room at the top and, when artifically illuminated, acts as a symbolic beacon for the DOM company.

House, Llewellyn Park, New Jersey. This project consists of two components: the renovation of a Georgian house designed in 1929 by Edgar Williams and the addition of alterations to the terraces and garden to accommodate a new tennis court and a new structure housing an indoor swimming pool. The renovation of the original structure responds to the owners' needs for more living space and less servants' quarters and to a feeling that the character of the original interior space was pompous. In reordering the interiors a syncopated counterpoint emerges between what appears to be, though is not necessarily, old and new. This is particularly vivid on the first floor where a new classically composed columnar screen wall encloses the living room. It can also be seen on the second floor where a sweeping diagonal ties together space in the principal part of the house with what was formerly the servants' wing.

The pool house is deliberately complex in its formal references—a place of recreation that responds to the character of the original house while at the same time taking on the character of a landscape feature. It is a kind of grotto or *nymphaeum* that marks a transition between the house, its terraces, and the garden. The palm tree columns that carry the terrace recall John Nash's at the Brighton Pavilion. These columns are used in a way similar to the manner in which this motif was used by Hans Hollein in a travel office in Vienna—to trigger appropriate and pleasant thoughts of sun-filled tropical islands. The tile walls give a subaqueous character to the room. The use of *faux*-marble pilasters of almost archaic character are a complement to the various high-tech strategies employed to capture solar heat and natural light and to open the pool to the garden.

STANLEY TIGERMAN

Stanley Tigerman was born in Chicago in 1930 and was educated at the Massachusetts Institute of Technology, the Institute of Design in Chicago, and the Yale University School of Architecture, from which he received the Bachelor of Architecture degree in 1960 and the Master of Architecture degree in 1961. From 1957 to 1959, he was a designer for Skidmore, Owings and Merrill in Chicago, from 1959 to 1961, an architectural draftsman with Paul M. Rudolph, New Haven, and from 1961 to 1962, the chief of design for Harry M. Weese in Chicago. From 1962 to 1964 he was a partner with Norman Koglin, Tigerman and Koglin, Chicago, and since 1964 has been a principal in Stanley Tigerman and Associates, Ltd., Chicago. From 1965 to 1971 he held an appointment as professor of architecture, University of Illinois at Chicago Circle, and has been visiting critic at numerous universities. Mr. Tigerman since 1966 has been the American correspondent of L'Architecture d'Aujourd'hui.

My interest in the relation of my work to classical architecture is demonstrated by my attempt to articulate roots in such a way that the buildings in which these allusions are at work are clearly related to the past, but not merely to historical phenomena. Instead, I view this relationship to the past as drawing upon a tradition of builders who have used the symbolic language of architecture—for example, symmetry, split symmetry, the orders, tri-partite divisions—and architectural methods in an "aedicular spirit" to relate buildings and their structures not only to human configuration but to the human spirit as well. Thus, I am less interested in directly tying my work to classical allusion on the totemic side of the history of architecture—the platonic, the ideal, the sense of perpetuity of life after death, the spirit of the ages—than I am to the aedicular theory which celebrates the human being as a frail finite creature rather than dismisses him as a being made less significant when seen in the light of perpetual values.

Nymeyer House Project Crete, Illinois, 1980. The house is located on a large tract of forested land. Its orientation is to the south in relation to a creek (which is sufficiently downhill from the table land so as to suggest orientation in that direction). The program for the project calls for a house for a family of six with a tennis court, swimming pool and guest house. The approach to the house is made on an entrance road through the forest which parts to reveal a drive-in courtyard, the top of which acts as a *belvedere*. The house is either entered informally in the center at the point of the garage rising up to a foyer which is axially related to the *belvedere*, or the house is approached ceremonially on a long ramp coming up to the point of entry at the inboard side of the same *belvedere*. Continuing up that

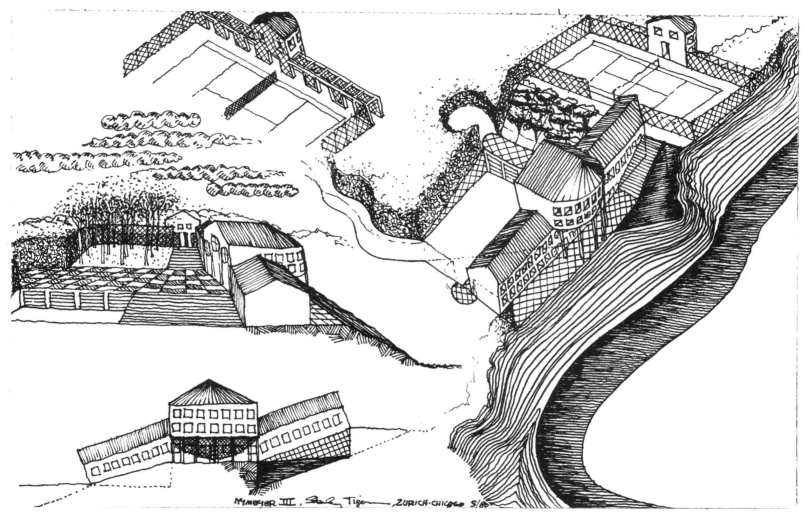

41. Tigerman, *Nymeyer House,* 1980, cat. 128.

ramp one finds a terraced garden screening a tennis court on the left, the tennis court being a continuation of the ceremonial entrance axis which then ultimately leads beyond the tennis court to a guest building at the very end of that long axis. The guest building itself is a diminution of the basic house but turned perpendicularly to it.

Various classical allusions are at work in the development of this project: 1) the suggestion of the Villa Emo by Andrea Palladio but skewed, 2) a relation to the face at Bomarzo suggested by the view past the terraced garden to the symmetrical façade of the tennis guest building, 3) a reference to Palladio's Basilica in Vincenza which is modestly alluded to by the faces used at column capitals which in turn are trabeated with triumphal arches. It is thought that the transformative qualities of the skewed building with its secret garden sufficiently masks direct allusion such that a new synthesis seems in evidence.

ROBERT VENTURI

Robert Venturi was born in Philadelphia, Pennsylvania, in 1925. He received the Bachelor of Arts and Master of Fine Arts degrees from Princeton University in 1947 and 1950, respectively. As the recipient of the Prix de Rome, *he was in residence at the American Academy in Rome from 1954 to 1956, returning there in 1966 as Architect-in-Residence. From 1957 to 1965, he was a faculty member at the University of Pennsylvania and was named Charlotte Shepherd Davenport Professor of Architecture at Yale University in 1966, a post he retained until 1970. He was a partner in the firm Venturi, Cope and Lippincott, Philadelphia, from 1958 to 1961 and in the firm, Venturi and Short, Philadelphia, from 1961 to 1964. He has been a partner with John Rauch since 1964 and with Mr. Rauch and Denise Scott Brown since 1967. The firm Venturi, Rauch and Scott Brown was represented in the 1980 Venice* Biennale.

JOHN RAUCH

John Rauch, born in Philadelphia in 1930, studied at Wesleyan University and at the University of Pennsylvania, receiving the Bachelor of Architecture degree from there in 1957. He became a partner with Robert Venturi in Philadelphia in 1964, joined by Denise Scott Brown in 1967. From 1967 to 1969 he was appointed as a lecturer at the University of Pennsylvania and in 1969–70 served as chairman of the Official Practice Committee, American Institute of Architects.

DENISE SCOTT BROWN

Denise Scott Brown was born Denise Lakofski in 'Nkana, Zambia, in 1931 and became a naturalized citizen of the U.S. in 1967. She holds the Master of City Planning degree and the Master of Architecture degree from the University of Pennsylvania. Ms. Scott Brown has taught at the School of Fine Arts, University of Pennsylvania, the School of Architecture and Urban Planning, UCLA, the College of Environmental Design, University of California at Berkeley, and Yale University School of Architecture. In 1967, she joined Venturi and Rauch, Philadelphia, as architect and planner and later became a partner in the firm where she is presently Partner-in-Charge of Urban Planning.

One way to talk about architecture and analyze where you are in it is to define it. Every architect works with a definition in mind even if he or she doesn't know it, or if it is not explicit; every generation of architects has its own definitions. Our current definition is architecture is shelter with symbols on it. Or, architecture is shelter with decoration on it.

For many architects this may be a shocking definition because definitions in the last seventy-five years have been put in spatial, technological, organic, or linguistic terms. Definitions of modern architecture never included ornament, nor did they explicitly refer to shelter. . . .

Ornament and symbolism—certainly applied ornament and the simple uses of association—have been ignored in architecture, or condemned—ornament equated with crime by Adolf Loos as long ago as 1906, and symbolism associated with discredited historical electicism; applique on shelter would have been considered superficial by theorists of the Modern movement and contrary to the industrial techniques integral to Modern architecture.

But we like emphasizing shelter in architecture thereby including function in our definition, and we like admitting symbolic rhetoric in our definition which is not integral with shelter thereby expanding the content of architecture beyond itself and freeing function to take care of itself.

[from Robert Venturi, "A Definition of Architecture as Shelter with Decoration on it, and Another Plea for a Symbolism of the Ordinary in Architecture," *L'Architecture d'Aujourd'hui,* no. 197 (June, 1978), pp. 7–8.]

42. Venturi, *A Country House Based on Mount Vernon,* façade, 1979, cat. 131.

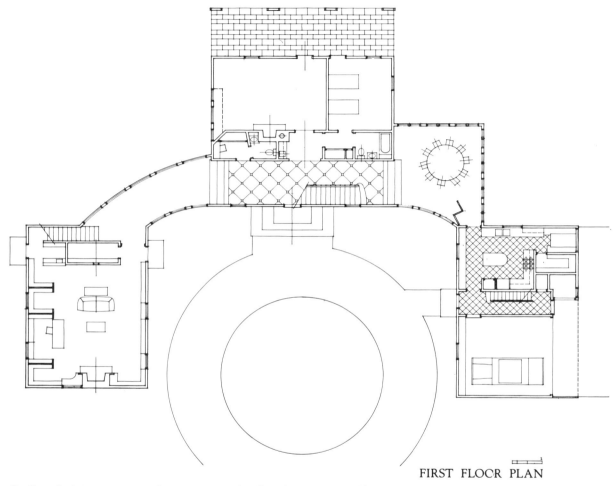

FIRST FLOOR PLAN

43. Venturi, *A Country House Based on Mount Vernon,* first-floor plan, 1979, cat. 134.

A Country House Based on Mount Vernon. This is a project for a house on a big site for a family that requested that it look like Mount Vernon to suit their rural way of life and to work as a background for their American antique furniture. Its plan accommodates particular requirements of the program; extra garages and facilities connected with maintenance of the estate are located beyond the house.

For Americans, Mount Vernon as the home of George Washington is highly charged with symbolism. It is hard to see the building as form as well as symbol, that is, to balance form and symbol in the way one usually does in the perception of a work of art. Reproducing it as a contemporary house is somewhat like Jasper Johns making a painting of the American flag.

We have purposely not made the building too correct because one can't be very accurate historically (our house contains many bathrooms and no slaves, for instance) and one shouldn't be— Bramante wasn't. There have been moments when architects have tended toward extreme historical accuracy—certain ecclesiastical architects in England in the nineteenth century and some domestic architects in America in the 1920s and 1930s, for example—but these movements became deadends historically, ingenious curiosities mostly, with limited application.

Our Mount Vernon is modified in certain ways. Some of the proportions are off. For instance, the length of the main block is short, the scale changes, with the side wings relatively large in scale, and the detailing is simplified, flattened, and therefore generalized. All of these modifications accommodate modern requirements of the program, reflect that the house is conceived all at once rather than grew over time, and exaggerate its symbolic content. Taking something familiar and making it slightly off can make its familiarity eloquent.

Knoll Showroom, New York, New York. Modern architecture dispensed with subtle color harmonies, historical allusion, ornament, and ambiguity. Knoll International is bringing them back in the form of a new 19,000 square foot showroom at 655 Madison Avenue.

I like elements which are hybrid rather than "pure," compromising rather than "clean," distorted rather than "straightforward."

The architects were selected after an extensive review of the work of many U.S. firms. Their selection will be viewed by some as an unexpected step for Knoll, but the company's history has been characterized by a continuing search for the most talented representatives of different approaches to design; in this instance, the design for a setting rather than for objects was involved. The architects were asked to create a stimulating environment on two floors of a 1950s glass and aluminum office building with the usual limitations of low ceilings and a grid of columns, to create a space where familiar things are seen in unfamiliar ways, from unexpected points of view, and to allow for continuing display changes of furnishings, fabrics and graphics.

The firm had previously designed major exhibitions for the Whitney and Smithsonian. They bring a feeling of theater to the occasion, which is appropriate, because going to a showroom can in fact be a theatrical event. The architect describes the scene as the elevators bring the visitor to the lower floor: "You are in a confined space with a theatrical effect. Neon splits the darkness and green hues emerge. Selected objects are spotted in light. Beyond you can glimpse a larger open space with bright ambient light and neutral background hues where furniture and fabrics may be seen and judged in a more familiar context." It is an eclectic parade of surprises. Off to the right, pouring through an opening from the floor above, comes a cascade of fabric gathered and draped in an old-fashioned way to resemble the folds in a Victorian ball gown. The parade of square columns is now a parade of round columns, explicitly ornamental. They flare out at the top of contain fixtures which spread ambient light from the ceiling. Monumentality and expediency are combined. The windows are covered with vertical panels of wood painted the same soft color as the whole outer area. Lines of daylight play within the panels. Encircling this "unmodern" indeterminacy is yet another ornamental device: a thin line of black paint which runs along the walls and columns almost at ceiling height. Borders did not belong to the aesthetic of the modern movement. The line contains and brings things together.

There is a sense of humor as well as a sense of history. The wall of fabric samples is faithfully duplicated with a *trompe l'oeil* wall of painted fabric beside it. Unorthodox things will be happening to some of the furniture as well. Years ago, the firm came to Knoll with an unheard-of request. They wanted to use a patterned fabric on a Mies chair. Knoll agreed to the idea.

The upper floor has a theatrical impact all its own, although for a different audience. It will be a simulation of an open plan office using Knoll's highly regarded Zapf and Stephens Systems. In addition, there is an explanatory exhibit dealing with some of Knoll's systems manufacturing processes. This level will also contain a luxuriously appointed conference room with Mies van der Rohe Brno chairs. It will be an almost pastel stylization of a classic boardroom, with walls of silk velvet. The room has a plastic luminous ceiling which projects the pattern of an eighteenth-century Robert Adam ceiling.

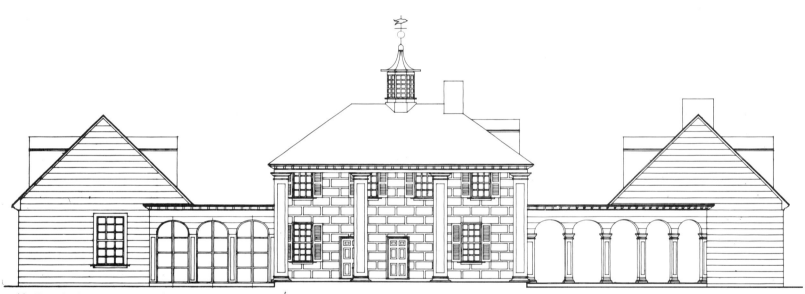

44. Venturi, *A Country House Based on Mount Vernon*, 1979, cat! 133.

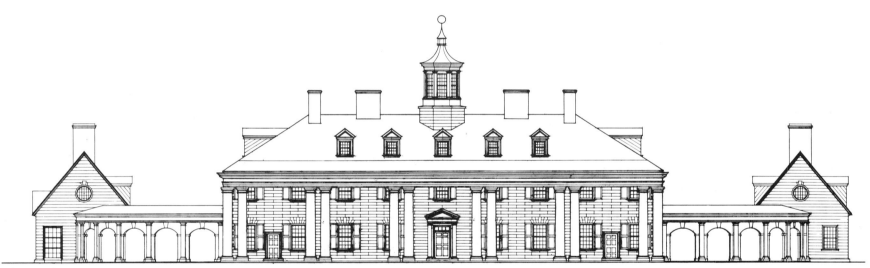

45. Greenberg, *A Connecticut Farm House*, 1980–81, cat. 31.

46. Harper, *Country House*, 1979–80, cat. 42.

CATALOGUE

THOMAS H. BEEBY

House of Poliphilos, designed 1977
Site: conceptual work for party-wall house
Program: investigation into the integration of modern construction and Palladian spatial form
Project Architect: Thomas H. Beeby
Color scheme: polychrome
Historical sources: Palladio, the modern movement, and Renaissance frescoes
    1. Model, 32 x 10 x 63 in. (Thomas H. Beeby with Kirsten Beeby, Phillip Castillo, Ralph Rangel, John Syvertsen; fig. 28)

Classical Imagery and City Form, a series of paintings
    2. *Summer,* 1979, magic marker on tracing paper, 35¼ x 35¼ in.

JOHN BLATTEAU

Additions and Renovations to the Bayonne Hospital, Bayonne, New Jersey, designed 1979
Project Principal: Robert Parsky
Project Designer: John Blatteau
Project Manager: Boyd Wolford
Renderers: John Blatteau, Ronni Rosenblatt and Stephen Bonitatibus
Contractor: Benedict Torcivia, Torcon Inc., Westfield, New Jersey
Full-scale wall model: Bob Barry, Harry Schwenk, Zerodec Megacorp, Chester, Pennsylvania; David J. Goldstein, Russell Cast Stone Company, Westmont, New Jersey (moulds)

    3. Model, polymerized plaster (Zerodec), 144 x 84 in.
    4. North elevation, photograph of colored drawing, 8 x 10 in.
    5. East elevation, photograph of colored drawing, 8 x 10 in.
    6. Construction photograph, 8 x 10 in.
    7. Construction photograph, 8 x 10 in.
    8. Construction photograph, 8 x 10 in.

Addition to the Holy Redeemer Hospital, Meadowbrook, Pennsylvania, designed 1981
Project Principal: Robert V. Cherry
Project Designer: John Blatteau
Project Manager: John Welsh
Renderers: John Blatteau, Ronni Rosenblatt and Stephen Bonitatibus
    9. Front elevation, watercolor on paper, 15 x 24 in.
    10. Side elevation, watercolor on paper, 15 x 15 in. (fig. 27)
    11. First-floor plan, photostat of line drawing, 8 x 10 in.
    12. Ground-floor plan, photostat of line drawing, 8 x 10 in.

PETER L. GLUCK AND ASSOCIATES

House, Lincoln, Massachusetts, designed 1977–80, executed 1980
Program: five-bedroom house for large family
Contractor: Keith Knudsen, High Falls, New York
Materials and method of contruction: wood frame
    13. Model, 30 x 24 x 10 in.
    14. South view, pencil on charcoal paper, 20 x 20 in. (fig. 29)
    15. North elevation, pencil on charcoal paper, 14 x 20 in.
    16. Section, pencil on charcoal paper, 14 x 20 in.
    17. First-floor plan, pencil on charcoal paper, 14 x 20 in.

MICHAEL GRAVES

House in Aspen, Colorado, 1978
18. Model, 16 x 16 x 6½ in.
19. Ground-floor plan, ink and colored pencil on yellow tracing paper, 24 x 24 in.
20. Façade from Hunter Creek, south, pen, ink and prismacolor on white tracing paper, 11 x 14 in. Lent by Gillian and Neil Levine, Cambridge, Massachusetts (fig. 30)
21. Façade from Roaring Fork River, west, ink and prismacolor on white tracing paper, 11 x 14 in. Lent courtesy of the Max Protetch Gallery, New York

Red River Valley Heritage Interpretive Center, Moorhead, Minnesota, 1980
22. First-floor plan, ink and colored pencil on paper, 17 x 22 in.
23. Site plan, ink and colored pencil on yellow tracing paper, 14½ x 14½ in.
24. Composite sketches, ink on illustration board, 30 x 30 in. (fig. 31)
25. Entrance façade, ink and watercolor on paper, 3½ x 8½ in. Lent courtesy of the Max Protetch Gallery, New York
26. Highway façade, ink and watercolor on paper, 3½ x 8½ in. Lent courtesy of the Max Protetch Gallery, New York
27. River façade, ink and watercolor on paper, 3½ x 8½ in. Lent courtesy of the Max Protetch Gallery, New York
28. Garden façade, ink and watercolor on paper, 3½ x 8½ in. Lent courtesy of the Max Protetch Gallery, New York

ALLAN GREENBERG

A Connecticut Farm House, designed 1979, executed 1980–82
Program: farmhouse on a large horse farm
Project Architect: James H. Jorgenson
Draftsmen: Richard Wies, Jacquelin Gargus, Eric Oliner, Robert Orr, Jacob Albert, J. M. B. McWilliams, Elizabeth Masters, Raymond L. Drouin, Ronni Rosenblatt
Modelmaker: Richard Wies
Contractor: Thomas P. Maguire, Inc.

Materials and method of construction: field-stone base, redwood siding, wood frame construction, brick chimneys
Color scheme: painted white with red stained shingles
Historical sources: eighteenth-century domestic architecture in Virginia, Maryland and Massachusetts; Palladio, San Michele and domestic architecture of North Italy.
29. Console model, Roma Plastilina, 5½ x 3½ x 2½ in.
30. First-floor plan, black line print, 30 x 42 in.
31. West elevation, black line print, 30 x 72 in. (fig. 45)
32. East elevation, black line print, 30 x 72 in.
33. Console detail, black line print, 30 x 42 in. (fig. 21)
34. Door, east side of main house, black line print, 30 x 42 in.
35. Parlor, interior elevations, black line print, 30 x 42 in.

ROBERT L. HARPER WITH CHARLES W. MOORE OF MOORE GROVER HARPER

Country House in New England, designed 1979–80, executed 1980–81
Program: a small house, primarily for summer use, with overflow space for visiting children and grandchildren
Project Architect: Robert L. Harper
Landscape Architect: Lester Collins
Project Manager: James Childress
Modelmaker: James Childress
Contractor: Gordon Oakes
Material and method of construction: brick veneer on main building, painted stucco on corner pavilions, slate roof, dry wall interior, dome of painted hardboard (made in sections) over living room
Color scheme: gray slate roof, stucco and brick in shades of pink
Historical source: Andrea Palladio
36. Model, 14¼ x 31¼ x 6 in.
37. Photograph of preliminary sketch by Charles Moore, 8 x 10 in.
38. Preliminary sketch, photograph of drawing, 8 x 10 in.
39. Preliminary drawing, plan and site plan, ink on yellow tracing paper, 14 x 17 in.
40. Composite drawing, main-floor plan and section, ink and air-brushed ink on illustration board, 26 x 28 in.

41. Interior dome, photograph, 14 x 11 in. (photographs 41, 42 by Robert L. Harper; fig. 17)
42. West façade, photograph, 11 x 14 in. (fig. 46)

PHILIP JOHNSON OF JOHNSON/BURGEE ARCHITECTS

Sugarland Office Park, Sugarland, Texas, designed 1980, to be executed 1981
Program: phased program of three-story suburban speculative office buildings
Draftsman: Bon-Hui UY
Materials and method of construction: poured concrete structure, brick exterior, limestone exterior details, built-up roof
Color scheme: red brick, sand-colored limestone
Client: Gerald D. Hines Interests
43. Perspective, photograph of drawing, 15¼ x 48 in.

The New Playhouse Theatre, Cleveland, Ohio, designed 1980–81, to be executed 1982
Program: one 650-seat dramatic theatre, one 200-seat experimental theatre plus support facilities for existing two theatres
Draftsman: Bon-Hui UY
Materials and method of construction: steel frame, brick exterior, slate roofs
Color scheme: match existing
Client: The Cleveland Playhouse
44. Perspective, photograph of drawing, 11¼ x 28 in. (fig. 32)

ROBERT MICHAEL KLIMENT AND FRANCES HALSBAND

Project for a Country House, 1980
Program: weekend house
Site: open fields in forested area
Draftsman: Alejandro Diez
Materials and method of construction: brick with wood windows, doors and trim, and a slate roof. The interiors are plaster, wallboard, and wood paneling, with painted or fabric finishes, and wood floors.
Historical source: eighteenth-century Wythe House, Williamsburg, Virginia

45. South and west sections, zipatone and colored pencil on line photographic reduction, 9 x 9 in.
46. Axonometric drawing of garden side, zipatone and colored pencil on line photographic reduction, 9 x 9 in. (fig. 47)
47. Axonometric drawing of entrance side, zipatone and colored pencil on line photographic reduction, 9 x 9 in.
48. Second-floor and attic plans, zipatone and colored pencil on line photographic reduction, 9 x 9 in.
49. Ground-floor plan, zipatone and colored pencil on line photographic reduction, 9 x 9 in.

A. G. Becker Incorporated, New York, New York, phase I completed 1980
Program: rebuilding three floors of offices for a stock brokerage and investment banking firm. Phase I consists of a set of reception and conference rooms at the elevator entrance of each floor.
Draftsman: Jack Esterson
Materials and method of construction: each entrance is marked by a portal of elm veneered columns. Through the portal, an octagonal cherry paneled reception room gives access to a suite of conference rooms.
Historical sources: classical elements and classically organized composition mark the development of the plans and ornamental system.
50. Axonometric drawing of the entrance, colored pencil on line photographic reproduction, 12 x 24 in.
51. Reception room, photograph, 16 x 20 in. (photographs 51–53 by Norman McGrath)
52. Conference room, photograph, 16 x 20 in.
53. Reception room and corridor, photograph, 16 x 20 in. (fig. 48)

EDWARD LEVIN

A Solar Greek-Revival House, 1980–81
Site: planned for Cambridge, New York
Program: a very small house (1,100 square feet) with studio for an architect and a potter. Passive solar energy devices (water-filled columns, trombe wall, solar greenhouse) are exaggerated to exploit their relationship to conventional architectural elements.

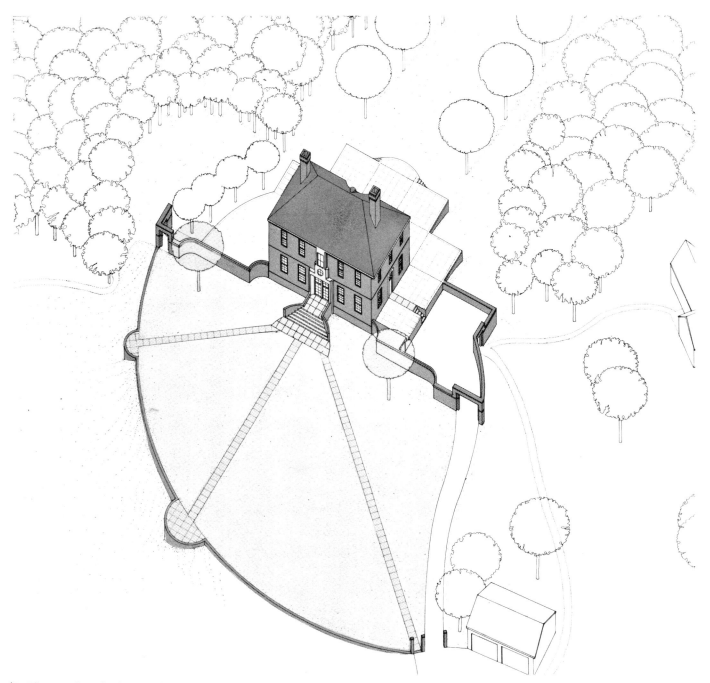

47. Kliment and Halsband, *Project for a Country House,* 1980, cat. 46.

Materials and method of construction: concrete masonry, wood joists and industrial sash, with stainless steel columns; structural clay tile, ceramic tile, quarry tile, and plaster interior finishes

Color scheme: grays of various tints

Historical source: standard "T"-type American Greek Revival house (ca. 1840)

Critical Assistance: Ellen K. Morris

54. Model, 11 x 11 x 11 in.
55. Isometric drawing, 1981, xerox with pencil and prismacolor pencil on Rives etching paper, 11 x 11 in. (fig. 26)
56. Ground-floor plan, 1981, xerox with pencil and prismacolor pencil on Rives etching paper, 11 x 11 in.

An American Standard Home, 1979

Site: planned for area near Charlottesville, Virginia

Program: this small house (1,800 square feet)—ostensibly a model home for a manufacturer of plumbing fixtures—is intended as a critique of the "Americanization" of European precedents, and as an attempt to recuperate a set of pre-modern devices for the representation of function.

Modelmaker: model painting by Ellen K. Morris

Materials and method of construction: porcelain-enameled steel panels over concrete masonry and structural clay tile, with wood joists and industrial sash; plaster, ceramic tile, structural clay tile, and polished concrete masonry interior finishes

Color scheme: façade: brick red with white sash and trim; other exterior surfaces: gray with gray sash

Historical sources: Maison de Mlle. Guimard (1775); Claude-Nicolas Ledoux and Pavilion IX (University of Virginia: 1821); Thomas Jefferson

Critical Assistance: Ellen K. Morris

57. Model, 15 x 15 x 10 in.
58. Expanded elevations, 1981, xerox with prismacolor pencil on Rives etching paper, 15 x 15 in.
59. Chamber-floor plan, 1981, ink on Strathmore Bristol, 21 x 21 in.
60. Entrance and garden front, 1979, ink on Strathmore Bristol, 21 x 21 in. (fig. 33)
61. Main-floor plan, 1979, ink on Strathmore Bristol, 21 x 21 in.
62. Pedestal sink, cast-iron, 20 x 24 x 30 in.

RODOLFO MACHADO AND JORGE SILVETTI

The Steps of Providence, 1979, Providence, Rhode Island

Site: conceptual work for the campus of the Rhode Island School of Design, Providence, Rhode Island

Program: a complex, multifunctional program which includes urban design, architecture and interiors with some new buildings and gardens, additions and remodelings

Design Assistants: Charles Crowley, Stephen Wanta

Draftsmen: Charles Crowley, James Favaro, Peter Lofgren, Stephen Wanta, Daniel Wheeler

63. General plan, ink on mylar, 40 x 40 in.
64. Frazier Terrace, garden steps, studio cloister (section), ink on mylar, 20 x 40 in.
65. Frazier Terrace, ink on mylar, 20 x 20 in.
66. Frazier Terrace, colored pencil on black line print, 20 x 20 in.
67. Memorial steps and Memorial Hall, ink on mylar, 20 x 20 in. (fig. 34)
68. Memorial steps and Memorial Hall, colored pencil on black line print, 20 x 20 in.
69. Garden steps, ink on mylar, 20 x 20 in.
70. Garden steps, colored pencil on black line print, 20 x 40 in.
71. Waterman Street entrance and the pool, ink on mylar, 20 x 20 in.
72. Market Square-Memorial steps, overview, ink on mylar, 20 x 40 in.

THE HENRY MELTZER GROUP

Door Surround, New York, New York, designed 1980, executed 1981

Architect: Henry L. Meltzer, New York; Henry L. Meltzer, Nick Ballard and Louis Vigorito Project Team

Draftsman: Louis Vigorito, January 1981

Modelmaker: Louis Vigorito, February 1981

Contractor: Morning Dew Woodworks, Inc., Brooklyn, New York

Materials: glass and painted wood

Client: The Henry Meltzer Group Incorporated, New York

73. Model, wood and paint, 37 x 24 x 4 in.
74. Section, photograph of drawing, 14 x 16 in.
75. Elevations, photograph of drawing, 14 x 16 in. (fig. 35)

CHARLES W. MOORE

Sammis Hall, Cold Spring Harbor, New York, designed 1978, executed 1980

Architects: Charles W. Moore, Glenn W. Arbonies, William H. Grover, Robert L. Harper, Steve Lloyd of Moore Grover Harper

Program: a guest house for Banbury Conference Center at Cold Spring Harbor Laboratory requiring sixteen bedrooms for scientists attending day or week-long research seminars, plus small meeting place

Project Architect: Glenn W. Arbonies
Architect of Record: Robert L. Harper
Draftsman: Steve Lloyd
Modelmaker: Spence Kass
Contractor: Tri-Con Construction, Port Washington, New York
Materials and method of construction: stucco over wood frame
Color scheme: white, pale terra cotta, light cool gray, warm pale neutral tones
Historical source: Palladio's Villa Poiana
Client: Cold Spring Harbor Laboratory

76. Model, 19⅛ x 19³/₁₆ x 9 in.
77. Interior perspective, drawing, 24 x 18 in.
78. North elevation, drawing, 11 x 16½ in. (reproduced on cover)
79. Section B-B, drawing, 14 x 17 in.
80. First-floor plan, drawing, 22 x 16⅝ in.

Cook House, 1980
81. Mock-up of an eave, painted wood, 33½ x 35¾ in. (Moore with Mark Simon)

Gund Investment Corporation, Princeton, New Jersey, 1979
82. Stenciled wall pattern, 32 x 40 in. (with Mark Simon; design consultant Tina Beebe)

CHRISTOPHER AND TIMOTHY MORRIS

Passive Solar Home, designed 1979, execution tentatively planned for the mid-1980s
Site: hypothetical; flat site with southern exposure

Program: to design a small energy efficient home of less than 1,750 square feet (capable of expansion) for less than $100,000. The dwelling is for a couple in their fifties whose three sons are grown and living elsewhere. However, accommodations for periodic overnight visits from one or two of the sons shall be provided.

Project Architects: Christopher and Timothy Morris
Draftsmen: Christopher and Timothy Morris
Modelmakers: Christopher and Timothy Morris
Materials and method of construction: wood frame, concrete block trombe wall, terne metal roofing, exposed plywood with aluminum dividers, lattice, acrylic and plate glass glazing, passive solar envelope system
Color scheme: flesh, lavender, green, slate gray and black
Historical sources: Palladian and Roman classicism
Client: Mr. and Mrs. George W. Morris

83. Sketchbook, 11 x 14 in.
84. Perspective, sepia print and prismacolor, 11 x 14 in.
85. South elevation, sepia print and prismacolor, 11 x 14 in. (fig. 36)
86. North elevation (decorated), sepia print and prismacolor, 11 x 14 in.
87. South elevation (decorated), sepia print and prismacolor, 11 x 14 in.
88. Heat gain flow, pencil on mylar, 11 x 14 in.
89. Expanded plan, pencil on mylar, 11 x 14 in.
90. Second-floor plan, pencil on mylar, 11 x 14 in.
91. Section, pencil on mylar, 11 x 14 in.

RICHARD B. OLIVER

Pittman Loft Remodeling, New York, New York, designed 1979, executed 1980

Program: conversion of an empty loft space into living accommodations for a couple without children. A large kitchen, pantry, bathroom, and closets/dressing rooms were requested in addition to the usual requirements of an apartment.

Project Architect: Richard Oliver
Materials and method of construction: gypsum wall board over metal studs, wood moldings, mosaic-tiled bathroom (completely tiled), marble vanity, tiled counters, wood and carpet floor covering

Color scheme: skylight: white; overall: cream and medium gray; classical walls: four shades of pink; bathroom: cream, gray and black tiles, marble vanity (verde issore)

Historical sources: no particular patternbooks. Source is an amalgam of buildings and interiors seen over the years. Particular exemplar: Soane and Adam.

Client: Robert and Sandy Pittman

92. Wall segment, wood and paint, 126 x 88 x 3 in. (constructed at SCMA by David Dempsey)

93. Axonometric drawing, ink on mylar, 21½ x 25 in. (fig. 37)

94. Floor plan, ink on mylar, 18 x 21½ in.

95. View of loft, photograph, 8 x 10 in. (Photograph by Tom Yee. Courtesy *House & Garden*. Copyright © 1981 by the Condé Nast Publications, Inc.)

STEVEN K. PETERSON AND BARBARA LITTENBERG

Competition Entry for the Re-design of Les Halles Quarter, Paris, 1979
Architects: Steven K. Peterson, Barbara Littenberg, David Cohn
Modelmakers: Lewis Jacobson, Paul Gleicher

96. Model, 34 x 48 x 7 in.

97. Perspective drawing, photograph with oil paint and magic marker, 24¼ x 22 in.

98. Perspective drawing, photograph with oil paint and magic marker, 24¼ x 22 in. (fig. 1)

99. Perspective drawing, photograph with oil paint and magic marker, 24¼ x 22 in.

100. Axonometric drawing, photograph with oil paint and magic marker, 42 x 34 in. (fig. 2)

101. Section, photograph with oil paint and magic marker, 13⅞ x 47½ in.

JAMES STEWART POLSHEK AND PARTNERS/PETER L. GLUCK AND ASSOCIATES, A JOINT VENTURE

Delafield Estate, Riverside, New York, 1980
Site: 10.41 acres of steeply sloping land with many large specimen trees and an existing house. The property is between an area of single-family homes and high-rise residential towers.
Program: thirty-three homes consisting of thirty new semiattached and detached houses and three homes within the structure of the existing house. Each house is approximately 3,500 square feet and is to include, among other amenities, an enclosed two-car garage and a maid's room.

Partner-in-Charge: Paul S. Byard
Design Team: James S. Polshek, Peter L. Gluck, Tyler H. Donaldson
Renderer: Tyler H. Donaldson
Materials and method of construction: wood frame, stained horizontal wood siding, stucco, and concrete roof tiles
Historical sources: the American Romantic Suburb as embodied in the surrounding Fieldston area of Riverside

102. Front elevation, colored pencil on board, 18 x 36 in.

103. Side elevation, colored pencil on board, 18 x 18 in.

104. Rear elevation, colored pencil on board, 18 x 36 in. (fig. 38)

105. Section, colored pencil on board, 18 x 18 in.

106. Site plan, colored pencil on board, 32 x 40 in.

THOMAS GORDON SMITH

Tuscan House and Laurentian House, Livermore, California, designed 1979, executed 1980
Program: two adjacent single-family houses on small lots, each with living room, kitchen-dining area, foyer, two bathrooms, three bedrooms and two-car garage; courts with vistas from one to another to extend sense of space
Project Architect: Thomas Gordon Smith
Draftsman: Thomas Gordon Smith
Contractor: George Jensen, Livermore, California
Materials and method of construction: wood frame on concrete slab; exterior: stucco with integral color, painted wood trim and ornament; interior: gypsum board and paint
Color scheme: walls: pastel blue, pink, yellow; trim: viridian, Venetian red, Windsor emerald, cerulean blue, chrome yellow
Historical sources: Pliny's description of Tuscan and Laurentian villas for ambience, Palladio's triumphal arches, Chamber's Doric order, Beaux-Arts-Maybeck polychromy, Salon at the Villa Foscari-Malcontenta for Tuscan living room, Viennese Secession for Laurentian fire place
Client: James and Demetra Wilson

107. Cutaway aerial perspective, ink and watercolor on Strathmore board, 30 x 36 in.

48. Kliment and Halsband, *A. G. Becker Inc.,* 1980, cat. 53.

108. Plans, ink on paper, 36 x 30 in.
109. Tuscan House, living room, photograph, 14 x 9½ in. (photographs 109–15 by Thomas Gordon Smith)
110. Tuscan House, foyer, photograph, 14 x 9½ in.
111. Laurentian House, foyer, photograph, 14 x 9½ in.
112. Laurentian House, living room, photograph, 9½ x 14 in.
113. Laurentian House, entablature (detail), photograph, 5 x 7 in.
114. Tuscan House, Laurentian House garage, view from the street, photograph, 9½ x 14 in.
115. Tuscan House, Laurentian House garage and house. View north from piazzetta, photograph, 14 x 9½ in. (fig. 39)

ROBERT A. M. STERN

DOM Headquarters, Brühl, Germany, 1980
Assistant-in-Charge: John Ike
Assistants: John Averitt, Terry Brown, Peter Pennoyer, Anthony Kohn
Model: John Ike
Perspective drawing: Terry Brown
116. Model, plastic, 32½ x 31½ x 15 in.
117. Ground-floor plan, section, east elevation, photograph of black line drawing on board, 17 x 22½ in.
118. Site plan, photograph of black line drawing on board, 17 x 22½ in.
119. Perspective, photograph of black line drawing on board, 32 x 42½ in. (fig. 40)
120. West elevation, typical plan, office floor, photograph of black line drawing on board, 17 x 22½ in.

Pool House, Llewellyn Park, New Jersey, designed 1980, currently under construction
121. Model, mixed media, 22⅛ x 34⅝ x 31 in.
122. Elevation, colored pencil on yellow tracing paper, 34 x 5½ in.
123. Column, colored pencil on yellow tracing paper, 9¼ x 6¼ in.
124. Perspective, colored pencil on yellow tracing paper, 25 x 15½ in.

STANLEY TIGERMAN

Nymeyer House, Crete, Illinois, designed 1980, currently under construction
Program: single-family residence
Associate-in-Charge: Robert Fugmon
Materials and method of construction: frame and stucco
Color scheme: P. D. F. Palette
Historical sources: Palladio's Villa Emo at Fanzolo and the face at Bomarzo
Client: Mr. and Mrs. Casey Nymeyer
125. Site plan, ink and prismacolor on tracing paper, 12 x 22 in. Lent courtesy of the Max Protetch Gallery, New York
126. Elevation, pencil and prismacolor on yellow tracing paper, 12 x 25¾ in. Lent courtesy of the Max Protetch Gallery, New York
127. Perspective, pencil on yellow tracing paper, 12 x 12 in. Lent courtesy of the Max Protetch Gallery, New York
128. Sketch, ink on paper, 5¼ x 8½ in. Lent courtesy of the Max Protetch Gallery, New York (fig. 41)
129. Elevation, pencil on yellow tracing paper, 12 x 12 in. Lent courtesy of the Max Protetch Gallery, New York
130. Sketch, ink on paper, 5¼ x 8¼ in. Lent courtesy of the Max Protetch Gallery, New York

ROBERT VENTURI, JOHN RAUCH & DENISE SCOTT BROWN

A Country House Based on Mount Vernon, 1979
Draftsman: James Timberlake
131. Front elevation, photograph of drawing, 8½ x 11 in. (fig. 42)
132. Side elevation, pencil on vellum, 31¾ x 48 in.
133. Rear elevation, pencil on vellum, 34½ x 48 in. (fig. 44)
134. First-floor plan, pencil on vellum, 34½ x 48 in. (fig. 43)

Knoll International, The New York Showroom, New York, New York, designed 1979, executed 1979–80
Program: 20,000 square feet, principally display space for furniture, office systems and textiles, with attendant office, conference and clerical space
Project Architects: Stanford Hughes, John Chase

Draftsmen: Stanford Hughes, Mark Hewitt, David Marohn,
Missy Maxwell
Modelmaker: Mark Hewitt
Contractor: All Building Corporation
Materials and method of construction: gypsum dry-wall interior
partitions, U.S. Gypsum Imperial System ceilings, custom
millwork
Client: Knoll International Inc.
135. Translucent ceiling, Knoll conference room, after
eighteenth-century ceiling by Robert Adam, photograph,
10 x 8 in. (photographs 135, 136 by Tom Crane; fig. 20)
136. Main display area, photograph, 8 x 10 in.
137. Ceiling design, lithograph, 6 x 10 in. Lent by Nan Swid
(reproduced on end papers)

MUSEUM VISITING COMMITTEE

In 1951, following a suggestion from the College's Board of Counsellors, a Visiting Committee to the Museum was formed by Mrs. John Wintersteen (Bernice McIlhenny '25) and the director of the Museum, Mr. Hitchcock. The members were chosen for their eminence as museum professionals or as collectors. Since that date the Museum's policies have been guided by this body. To them is due considerable credit for the enlargement of interest in the collection and for the many important gifts which have come to it.

Current Members

Mrs. Priscilla Cunningham (Priscilla Cunningham '58), Chairman
David S. Brooke
Mrs. Leonard Brown
Charles E. Buckley
Mrs. Malcolm G. Chace, Jr. (Beatrice Oenslager '28)
Mrs. Jerome Cohen (Joan Lebold '54)
Colin Eisler
Mrs. John R. Jakobson (Barbara Petchesky '54)
C. Douglas Lewis, Jr.
Dorothy C. Miller '25, Hon. L.H.D. '59 (Mrs. Holger Cahill)
Elizabeth Mongan
Mrs. John O'Boyle (Nancy Millar '52)
Mrs. James E. Pollak (Mabel Brown '27)
Sue Welsh Reed (I. Sue Welsh '58)
Morton I. Sosland
Mrs. Morton I. Sosland (Estelle Glatt '46)
Mrs. Alfred R. Stern (Joanne Melniker '44)
Mrs. Charles Lincoln Taylor (Margaret R. Goldthwait '21)
Enid Silver Winslow (Enid Silver '54)
Mrs. John Wintersteen (Bernice McIlhenny '25)

Former Members

Jere Abbott: 1965–1974
W. G. Russell Allen: 1951–1955
Mrs. Ralph F. Colin (I. Georgia Talmey '28): 1951–1970
Mrs. John Cowles (Elizabeth M. Bates '22): 1951–1954
Charles Cunningham: 1963–1979
Mrs. Charles C. Cunningham (Eleanor A. Lamont '32): 1951–1960
Mrs. Henry T. Curtiss (Mina Kirstein '18): 1963–1969
Dorothy Dudley (Mrs. John M. Ginnelly): 1969–1975
Selma Erving '27: 1966–1980
Ernest Gottlieb: 1956–1969
Philip Hofer: 1951–1968
Mrs. Sigmund Kunstadter (Maxine Weil '24): 1969–1977
Sigmund W. Kunstadter: 1976
Mrs. Maurice Lazarus (Nancy Stix '42): 1951–1969
Stanley Marcus: 1955–1962
A. Hyatt Mayor: 1969–1977
Agnes Mongan '29, Hon. L.H.D. '41: 1951–1970
Beaumont Newhall: 1974–1977
James Thrall Soby: 1951–1979

MUSEUM STAFF

Charles Chetham, Director, Chief Curator, Curator of Sculpture
Betsy B. Jones, Associate Director, Curator of Painting
Christine Swenson, Assistant Curator of Prints and Drawings
Linda Muehlig, Assistant Curator of Painting
Patricia Anderson, Curatorial Assistant
Kathryn Woo, Assistant for Administration
Louise Laplante, Registrar
David Dempsey, Preparator
Michael Goodison, NEA Intern
Martha Krom, NEA Intern
Constance Ellis, Assistant for Publicity and Events
Jean Mair, Archivist
Wilda Craig, Receptionist, Museum Members Secretary
Janice St. Laurence, Receptionist
Drusilla Kuschka, Secretarial Assistant
Steven Kern, Preparator's Assistant